Project Management Solutions Ltd.

# Passing the PMP Exam
## Learner Guide

### First Edition
### Dorcas M. T. Cox, PMP

iUniverse, Inc.
New York   Bloomington

Passing the PMP Exam
Learner Guide

iUniverse books may be ordered through booksellers or by contacting:

iUniverse
1663 Liberty Drive
Bloomington, IN 47403
www.iuniverse.com
1-800-Authors (1-800-288-4677)

ISBN: 978-1-4401-9366-8 (pbk)
ISBN: 978-1-4401-9367-5 (ebk)

Printed in the United States of America

iUniverse rev. date: 12/10/2009

## ABOUT PROJECT MANAGEMENT SOLUTIONS LTD.

Project Management Solutions Ltd. is a privately owned company committed to providing quality project management training, and consulting solutions based on the project management body of knowledge. Our products and services are designed to improve organizational, group, and individual performance. Our team of professionals is headed by Dorcas M. T. Cox with over fourteen years of consecutive experience in human resources management, instructional design, and project management. Dorcas has worked for government and multinational companies, a college/ university, as a consultant, and has studied, lived and worked in North America, and Canada.

## WELCOME MESSAGE

Welcome to the Passing the PMP Exam course. This course is taught by Dorcas M. T. Cox, PMP and is aimed at those whose goal is to achieve the internationally recognized Project Management Professional (PMP) designation.

This course pairs the Project Management Body of Knowledge (PMBOK Guide) theory and best practices with practical exercises. Course content is based on the (PMBOK Guide) fourth edition which is specifically covered in the Project Management Professional (PMP) exam.

You will participate in practical exercises, quizzes and study test taking tips using Project Management Institute's (PMI) terminology to prepare you to write the rigorous PMP exam. By the end of the class you will gain the knowledge and confidence needed to pass the PMP examination the first time you sit it.

## COURSE FEATURES

The Passing the PMP Exam course is customized to include the following features
* forty hours of project management instruction accepted by PMI as formal educational requirements for eligibility to sit the PMP exam
* review of PMP examination requirements, including test taking techniques
* review of definitions, terms, and processes found in the PMBOK Guide, and
* in depth knowledge of the PMBOK Guide's process groups, knowledge areas and area of professional and social responsibility.

## OUR BENEFITS

Project Management Solutions Ltd. provides the following benefits through the products, and services that we offer. You will
* learn, and demonstrate competence in the application of project management techniques
* maximize efficiency, and effectiveness on, and off of the job
* prepare to pass the PMP examination, and
* gain, and maintain a competitive edge in project management.

## LEARNER GUIDE

This learner guide serves as a companion guide to the PMBOK Guide and includes the information needed to help you navigate the course with success.

Familiarize yourself with the following components of this guide

- measurement, and evaluation
- learner responsibilities
- lecturer/instructor responsibilities
- about the Project Management Institute (PMI), and
- about the Project Management Professional (PMP) Exam.

## MEASUREMENT AND EVALUATION

Individual and Group Exercises and or Assignments

- This course is designed to give you the opportunity to complete individual, small group, and full class exercises, and assignments.
- Some instructions for completing these exercises may be found in your learner guide, others may be given to you by your instructor.
- These exercises and assignments are intended to help you to confirm your understanding of the content, and assist you in taking steps to apply learning on the job.

Tests

- Three different multiple choice tests will be administered to you at different points throughout the duration of the course.
- Time will be allocated during the course to allow you to complete the test questions in class without the assistance of your note books or study guide. Tests will be scored and discussed in class. This method gives you the opportunity to assess your understanding of the learning content associated with the course. Your course instructor will record test grades, and return tests to you for your records.
- This method of assessment makes you aware of the areas of the course material that require more dedicated time, study, or further discussion, and or explanation.

## MEASUREMENT AND EVALUATION

Written Project Assignment

- A written project assignment gives you, and your instructor the opportunity to determine whether you have developed the ability to fully apply the knowledge and skill learned in the course in a real life project scenario.
- You will be asked to complete a written assignment using a real life project scenario that you are directly involved in. The requirement for successful completion of this exercise is the demonstrated use of all project management concepts previously learnt in the course. Total point allocation for this assignment – Fifty (50) points.
- Your instructor will inform you of the deadline for completing this assignment.

End of Program Evaluation

- You will be asked to assess your overall satisfaction with the Passing the PMP Exam course as well as your intention to apply what you learnt on the job.
- Completed learner evaluations are important to Project Management Solutions Ltd. Your feedback is used to assess the effectiveness of the course, and allow for further development.
- These assessments are completely confidential, and will only be used to assist in assessing the course effectiveness.

## LEARNER RESPONSIBILITIES

It is important that you are aware of your role and the instructor's expectations for you to ensure your success as you progress through the Passing the PMP Exam course.

The table below gives you a quick summary of your key responsibilities. Take some time to review the table below before you continue to progress throughout the remainder of this learner guide. Your instructor will be prepared to answer any questions that you may have regarding any of the information presented.

| Role | Before | During | After |
|------|--------|--------|-------|
| Learner | • Approach the program with a clear and open mind.<br>• Agree to the terms and guidelines of the Passing the PMP Exam course. | • Review the learner guide and other supplemental reading material that may be issued to you by your instructor.<br>• Complete all required components of the Passing the PMP Exam course including but not limited to all individual and or group exercises, individual and or group written case assignment, tests and end of program evaluation.<br>• Focus on the learning and reduce distractions.<br>• Prepare for class sessions in advance.<br>• Actively participate, ask questions and provide feedback.<br>• Seek out other learning opportunities, ask questions that relate to the learning content, take advantage of your instructor's expertise and be open to feedback.<br>• Have fun and enjoy the learning process. | • Apply the knowledge and skills that you learnt from the course on the job.<br>• Take advantage of additional learning opportunities.<br>• Complete post-program questionnaire. |

## INSTRUCTOR'S RESPONSIBILITIES

Your instructor plays a key role in guiding you through the course. The information about your instructor's responsibilities is listed below for easy reference.

| Role | Before | During | After |
|------|--------|--------|-------|
| Instructor | • Review program content and all relevant course material in preparation for the respective class.<br>• Agree to the terms and guidelines that relate to the Passing the PMP Exam course. | • Arrange access to required learning activities and resources.<br>• Conduct in class sessions for the Passing the PMP Exam course.<br>• Provide guidance and answer questions.<br>• Solicit input and give feedback.<br>• Assist with the removal of barriers to learning and distractions that may be present in class.<br>• Manage time wisely and navigate learners through the course.<br>• Record all quiz grades, mark all written case assignments and complete all necessary record keeping requirements. | • Remain available as an external resource to learners if and where necessary. |

## ABOUT THE PROJECT MANAGEMENT INSTITUTE

The Project Management Institute (PMI) is the leading membership association for the project management professional with nearly two hundred and twenty thousand members in over one hundred and sixty countries. The Project Management Institute (PMI) is actively engaged in advocacy for the profession, setting professional standards, conducting research, and providing access to a wealth of information, and resources. The Project Management Institute (PMI) also promotes career, and professional development, and offers certification, networking and community involvement opportunities.

The Project Management Institute (PMI) has advanced the careers of practitioners for more than thirty seven years.

## ABOUT THE PMP CREDENTIAL

The Project Management Professional (PMP) credential is the project management profession's most recognized and respected global credential. To obtain a PMP credential, candidates must satisfy education, and experience requirements, agree to adhere to a professional code of conduct, and pass the PMP examination. The PMP certification program supports the global community of project management practitioners, and is designed to objectively assess, and measure professional knowledge. The Project Management Institute's (PMI) PMP credential offers individuals a wide range of important benefits. The PMP designation demonstrates to employers, and other stakeholders that the holder posses a solid foundation of experience, and education in project management. The PMI certification program is the first professional certification program of its kind to receive the ISO 9001 certification, globally recognized mark of a quality management system.

Individuals who hold the PMP credential command salaries that are seventeen point two percent higher on average than their non-credentialed counterparts as a result of the reputation that the PMP has earned over the past twenty two years.

# CONTENTS

# INTRODUCTION

# INTRODUCTION

The check-in meeting between you and your instructor is a critical part of the learning process. This first check-in meeting is intended for your course instructor to provide you with the essential information that you need to know to successfully complete the Passing the PMP Exam course. This meeting is a great opportunity for your instructor to get to know you and to understand your expectations as it relates to the course.

## OBJECTIVES

- define the components of the Passing the PMP Exam course.
- state the objective of the Passing the PMP Exam course.
- list and describe the methods of measurement and evaluation contained in the components of the Passing the PMP Exam course.
- define the role of the instructor as it pertains to the Passing the PMP Exam course.
- describe the responsibilities of the instructor before, during and after the course and the intended impact of this role on you, the learner.
- explain PMI's eligibility requirements for submitting an application to sit the PMP exam.
- explain how candidates to sit the exam are required to document experience as a part of the application submission process.
- explain the PMP credential fees and process for submitting the online application request to sit the PMP exam.

## REQUIREMENTS TO COMPLETE SECTION

Successful completion of this section is achieved by obtaining oral sign off from learner and instructor.

## TIME REQUIRED

Thirty minutes for the duration of the meeting.

## SIGN-OFF

Oral sign off for completion of this meeting will be completed by the learner and instructor.

## RESOURCES

The following outlines the resources that you will need to complete this section:
- Project Management Professional (PMP) Credential Handbook – revised June 2009

## INSTRUCTIONS

Follow the steps below to complete this section.

| Step | Action |
|------|--------|
| 1 | Read the instructions in this section. |
| 2 | Read the respective pages in the Passing the PMP Exam course learner guide so that you are familiar with the features and benefits and your instructor's responsibilities to assist you in successfully working through the course. |
| 3 | You are ready to begin. |
| 4 | Give oral sign off to your instructor upon completion of the meeting. |

## YOUR COURSE INSTRUCTOR WILL MEET WITH YOU AND DO THE FOLLOWING.

- Welcome you to the Passing the PMP Exam course.
- Invite you to use the "Check-In" section of your learner guide during the meeting.
- State the objectives of the course.
- Inform you of your role as learner for the course.
- Inform you of their role as instructor for the course.
- Listen to your expectations it relates to the Passing the PMP Exam course.
- Discuss the course evaluation requirements.
- Answer any questions that you may have regarding the course.
- Review the course outline along with you.
- Agree to specific dates, times and method for future check ins with you.
- Mention the requirement to have you complete the Student Contact Sheet.
- Issue a copy of the Student Contact Sheet for your completion.
- Ask you if you have any questions.

## DEBRIEFING QUESTIONS

The following are some questions that your instructor may ask you to summarize the meeting, stimulate dialogue and confirm your overall understanding of the concepts that were discussed. These debriefing questions are included here in your learner guide so that you are aware of the meeting format in advance and have a general idea of what to expect.

- What do you understand the requirements are to successfully complete the Passing the PMP Exam course?
- How long is the duration of the Passing the PMP Exam course?
- What are PMI's requirements for submitting an application to sit the PMP examination?
- When should you begin to compile your application material for submission to PMI?
- What are your concerns about the Passing the PMP Exam course?
- How do you feel about the Passing the PMP Exam course?

# INTRODUCTION TO PROJECT MANAGEMENT

**A**FTER STUDYING THIS CHAPTER, YOU SHOULD BE ABLE TO

- define the three characteristics of a project.
- explain the three things that projects can create.
- define project management.
- list and describe the project management process groups.
- list and describe the project management knowledge areas.
- align the project management knowledge areas to the respective process groups.
- describe portfolio management.
- describe program management.
- explain the link between projects and strategic planning.
- state the purpose of the project management office.
- differentiate between project management and operations management.
- define the project life cycle and explain the characteristics.
- differentiate between a project phase and a process group.
- define stakeholders.
- list the persons and or groups internal and or external to the organization that fit the definition of a stakeholder.
- explain the importance of properly identifying stakeholders at the outset of the project.
- Differentiate between a functional, weak matrix, balanced matrix, strong matrix and projectized organization structure.

**A**S YOU READ THIS CHAPTER, BE SURE THAT YOU UNDERSTAND THE FOLLOWING TERMS AND IDEAS.

- Sponsor
- Project Team
- Project Management Knowledge Areas
- Portfolio Management
- Operations Management
- Functional Organization

- Project Manager
- Functional Manager
- Project Management Process Groups
- Strategic Planning
- Project Life Cycle
- Weak Matrix
- Strong Matrix

- Customers/Users
- PMBOK Guide
- Project
- Project Management
- Program Management
- Project Management Office
- Project Phase
- Balanced Matrix
- Projectized Organization

## REQUIREMENTS TO COMPLETE SECTION

To successfully complete this section, you must
- complete the learning check
- complete the learning in action requirements
- complete the on-the-job activities, and
- answer brain teaser questions assigned by instructor.

## TIME REQUIRED

This section is included as a part of unit one. One week is allotted for successful completion of unit one.

## SIGN-OFF

Sign off for this section will be completed by the instructor.

## RESOURCES

The following outlines the resources that you will need to complete this section
- PMBOK Guide fourth edition, sections 1.1 – 3.7.2.
- Heldman, fifth edition chapter 1.

## INSTRUCTIONS

Follow the steps below to complete this section and learning check.

| Step | Action |
|------|--------|
| 1 | Read the material in this section including the pages indicated in the resources section above. |
| 2 | Write down any notes or questions that you may wish to discuss with your instructor during your scheduled class. |
| 3 | Discuss any questions and/or concerns with your instructor. |
| 4 | Complete the learning in action, brain teaser and/or on-the-job activities presented by the instructor. |

Define the three characteristics of a project

_____

_____

_____

_____

_____

Explain the three things that a project can create

_____

_____

_____

_____

_____

_____

Define project management

_____

_____

_____

_____

_____

List and describe the project management process groups

| Name of Process Group | Description of Process Group |
|---|---|
|  |  |
|  |  |
|  |  |
|  |  |
|  |  |
|  |  |
|  |  |
|  |  |
|  |  |
|  |  |
|  |  |
|  |  |

| Name of Process Group | Description of Process Group |
|---|---|
| | |
| | |
| | |
| | |
| | |
| | |
| | |
| | |
| | |
| | |
| | |
| | |

List and describe the project management knowledge areas

| Name of Knowledge Area | Description of Knowledge Area |
|---|---|
| | |
| | |
| | |
| | |
| | |
| | |
| | |
| | |
| | |
| | |
| | |
| | |
| | |
| | |
| | |
| | |
| | |
| | |
| | |

| Name of Knowledge Area | Description of Knowledge Area |
|---|---|
| | |
| | |
| | |
| | |
| | |
| | |
| | |
| | |
| | |
| | |
| | |
| | |
| | |
| | |
| | |
| | |
| | |
| | |
| | |
| | |
| | |
| | |
| | |
| | |
| | |
| | |
| | |
| | |
| | |
| | |
| | |
| | |
| | |
| | |
| | |
| | |
| | |

Align the project management knowledge areas to the respective process groups

Fill in the blank to identify the process group that is aligned to the respective knowledge area

| Project Integration Management Primary Tasks | Project Management Process Group |
|---|---|
| Develop Project Charter | |
| Develop Project Management Plan | |
| Direct and Manage Project Execution | |
| Monitor and Control Project Work | |
| Integrated Change Control | |
| Close Project | |

| Project Scope Management Primary Tasks | Project Management Process Group |
|---|---|
| Collect Requirements | |
| Scope Definition | |
| Create WBS | |
| Scope Verification | |
| Scope Control | |

| Project Time Management Primary Tasks | Project Management Process Group |
|---|---|
| Activity Definition | |
| Activity Sequencing | |
| Activity Resource Estimating | |
| Activity Duration Estimating | |
| Schedule Development | |
| Schedule Control | |

| Project Cost Management Primary Tasks | Project Management Process Group |
|---|---|
| Cost Estimating | |
| Cost Budgeting | |
| Cost Control | |

| Project Quality Management Primary Tasks | Project Management Process Group |
|---|---|
| Quality Planning | |
| Perform Quality Assurance | |
| Perform Quality Control | |

| Project Human Resources Management Primary Tasks | Project Management Process Group |
|---|---|
| Human Resources Planning | |
| Acquire Project Team | |
| Develop Project Team | |
| Manage Project Team | |

| Project Communications Management Primary Tasks | Project Management Process Group |
|---|---|
| Identify Stakeholders | |
| Communications Planning | |
| Information Distribution | |
| Manage Stakeholders | |
| Report Performance | |

| Project Communications Management Primary Tasks | Project Management Process Group |
|---|---|
| Risk Management Planning | |
| Risk Identification | |
| Qualitative Risk Analysis | |
| Quantitative Risk Analysis | |
| Risk Response Planning | |
| Risk Monitoring and Control | |

| Project Procurement Management Primary Tasks | Project Management Process Group |
|---|---|
| Plan Procurement | |
| Conduct Procurement | |
| Administer Procurements | |
| Close Procurements | |

**Describe portfolio management**

_____

_____

_____

_____

_____

**Describe program management**

_____
_____
_____
_____
_____

**Explain the link between projects and strategic planning**

_____
_____
_____
_____
_____

**State the purpose of the project management office**

_____
_____
_____
_____
_____

**Differentiate between projects and operational management**

| Projects | Operational Management |
|---|---|
|  |  |
|  |  |
|  |  |
|  |  |
|  |  |
|  |  |
|  |  |
|  |  |
|  |  |

**Define the project life cycle and explain the characteristics**

_____
_____
_____
_____
_____

**Projects vary in size and complexity. No matter how large or small, simple or complex, all projects can be mapped to a life cycle structure. What is this structure?**

_____
_____
_____
_____
_____

**Differentiate between project phases and process groups**

| Project Phases | Process Groups |
|---|---|
|  |  |
|  |  |
|  |  |
|  |  |
|  |  |
|  |  |
|  |  |
|  |  |

**Definition of stakeholders**

_____
_____
_____
_____

**List the persons or groups internal and or external to the organization that fit the definition of a stakeholder**

| Person or Group | Definition |
|---|---|
|  |  |
|  |  |
|  |  |
|  |  |
|  |  |
|  |  |
|  |  |
|  |  |
|  |  |
|  |  |
|  |  |
|  |  |
|  |  |
|  |  |
|  |  |
|  |  |
|  |  |
|  |  |
|  |  |
|  |  |
|  |  |
|  |  |
|  |  |

**Differentiate between a functional, weak matrix, balanced matrix, strong matrix and projectized organization structure**

| Name of Organizational Structure | Description |
|---|---|
|  |  |
|  |  |
|  |  |
|  |  |
|  |  |
|  |  |
|  |  |

| Name of Organizational Structure | Description |
|---|---|
| | |
| | |
| | |
| | |
| | |
| | |
| | |
| | |
| | |
| | |
| | |
| | |
| | |
| | |

## LEARNING IN ACTION AND/OR ON-THE-JOB ACTIVITIES

The following is an activity that may be completed individually or as a small group. This activity is intended to assess your comprehension and application of the material that was previously covered. Answer the questions below and make some notes in the space provided.

Consider what happened on the last project that you were involved in or managed.

What factors contributed to the success of the project?

_____

_____

_____

_____

_____

Which of the factors contributing to the success of the project relate to the concepts covered in this section?

_____

_____

_____

_____

_____

What tasks that relate to the material previously covered, helped you to successfully complete your project?

_____

_____

_____

_____

_____

List and describe the areas of the project where you experienced challenges?

_____

_____

_____

_____

_____

What factors contributed to this?

_____

_____

_____

_____

_____

Given what you learned about the areas covered in the previous section, what would you do differently in your next project?

_____

_____

_____

_____

What tasks did you neglect that may have contributed to a more successful outcome?

_____

_____

_____

_____

_____

## THINGS THAT I NEED TO WORK ON

The following are things that I need to work on to be proficient in the concepts covered in this chapter.

_____

_____

_____

_____

_____

_____

_____

_____

_____

_____

# PROJECT INITIATION

## AFTER STUDYING THIS CHAPTER, YOU SHOULD BE ABLE TO

- State the purpose of project initiation and list the two processes that are included as a part of project initiation.
- explain the purpose of the project charter.
- List and describe the steps to be completed when creating a project charter.
- explain who signs off on the project charter and explain the importance of obtaining this sign-off.
- Explain the purpose of identifying the stakeholders.
- list and describe the steps to be completed when identifying stakeholders.

## AS YOU READ THIS CHAPTER, BE SURE THAT YOU UNDERSTAND THE FOLLOWING TERMS AND IDEAS.

- Initiating Process
- Project Charter
- Identifying Stakeholders

## REQUIREMENTS TO COMPLETE SECTION

To successfully complete this section, you must
- complete the learning check
- complete the learning in action requirements
- complete the on-the-job activities, and
- answer brain teaser questions assigned by instructor.

## TIME REQUIRED

This section is included as a part of unit two. One week is allotted for successful completion of unit two.

## SIGN-OFF

Sign off for this section will be completed by the instructor.

## RESOURCES

The following outlines the resources that you will need to complete this section
- PMBOK Guide fourth edition, sections 4.1 and 10.1.
- Heldman, fifth edition chapter 2.

## INSTRUCTIONS

Follow the steps below to complete this section and learning check.

| Step | Action |
|---|---|
| 1 | Read the material in this section including the pages indicated in the resources section above. |
| 2 | Write down any notes or questions that you may wish to discuss with your instructor during your scheduled class. |
| 3 | Discuss any questions and/or concerns with your instructor. |
| 4 | Complete the learning in action, brain teaser and/or on-the-job activities presented by the instructor. |

## THE PROJECT CHARTER

Fill in the blanks with the appropriate descriptor

| Begin With | The Contract |
|---|---|
| 1. Contract (Where Applicable) | _____<br>_____<br>_____<br>_____ |
| 2. Project Statement of Work | **Project Statement of Work**<br>_____<br>_____<br>_____<br>_____ |
| 3. Enterprise Environmental Factors | **Enterprise Environmental Factors**<br>_____<br>_____<br>_____<br>_____ |
| 4. Organizational Process Assets | **Organizational Process Assets**<br>_____<br>_____<br>_____<br>_____ |
| 5. Business Case | **Business Case**<br>_____<br>_____<br>_____<br>_____ |
| **Method** | **Expert Judgment** |
| 1. Use Expert Judgment | _____<br>_____<br>_____<br>_____ |

## THE PROJECT CHARTER

Fill in the blanks with the appropriate descriptor

| Result | Project Charter |
|---|---|
| 1. Project Charter | |

## IDENTIFYING STAKEHOLDERS

Fill in the blanks with the appropriate descriptor

| **Begin With** | **Project Charter** |
|---|---|
| 1. Project Charter | _____ |
|  | _____ |
|  | _____ |
|  | _____ |
| 2. Procurement Documents | **Procurement Documents** |
|  | _____ |
|  | _____ |
|  | _____ |
|  | _____ |
| 3. Enterprise Environmental Factors | **Enterprise Environmental Factors** |
|  | _____ |
|  | _____ |
|  | _____ |
|  | _____ |
| 4. Organizational Process Assets | **Organizational Process Assets** |
|  | _____ |
|  | _____ |
|  | _____ |
|  | _____ |
| **Method** | **Expert Judgment** |
| 1. Use Expert Judgment | _____ |
|  | _____ |
|  | _____ |
| 2. Stakeholder Analysis | **Stakeholder Analysis** |
|  | _____ |
|  | _____ |
|  | _____ |

## IDENTIFYING STAKEHOLDERS

Fill in the blanks with the appropriate descriptor

| Result | |
|---|---|
| | **Stakeholder Register** <br> _____ <br> _____ <br> _____ <br> _____ |
| 1. Stakeholder Register | |
| 2. Stakeholder Management Strategy | **Stakeholder Management Strategy** <br> _____ <br> _____ <br> _____ <br> _____ |

**State the purpose of project initiation and list the two processes that occur as a part of project initiation**

_____

_____

_____

_____

_____

**Explain the purpose of the project charter**

_____

_____

_____

_____

_____

**List and describe the steps to be completed when completing the project charter**

_____

_____

_____

_____

_____

**Explain who signs off on the project charter and explain the importance of obtaining this sign off**

_____

_____

_____

_____

_____

**Explain the purpose of identifying the stakeholders**

_____

_____

_____

_____

**List and describe the steps to be completed when identifying stakeholders**

_____

_____

_____

_____

_____

## LEARNING IN ACTION AND/OR ON-THE-JOB ACTIVITIES

The following is an activity that may be completed individually or as a small group. This activity is intended to assess your comprehension and application of the material that was previously covered. Answer the questions below and make some notes in the space provided.

Consider what happened on the last project that you were involved in or managed.

What factors contributed to the success of the project?

_____

_____

_____

_____

_____

Which of the factors contributing to the success of the project relate to the concepts covered in this section?

_____

_____

_____

_____

_____

What tasks that relate to the material previously covered, helped you to successfully complete your project?

_____

_____

_____

_____

_____

List and describe the areas of the project where you experienced challenges?

_____

_____

_____

_____

_____

What factors contributed to this?

_____

_____

_____

_____

Given what you learned about the areas covered in the previous section, what would you do differently in your next project?

_____

_____

_____

_____

_____

What tasks did you neglect that may have contributed to a more successful outcome?

_____

_____

_____

_____

_____

## THINGS THAT I NEED TO WORK ON

The following are things that I need to work on to be proficient in the concepts covered in this chapter.

_____

_____

_____

_____

_____

_____

_____

_____

_____

_____

# PROJECT PLANNING

- explain the purpose of the project plan document.
- list and describe the subsidiary documents that are included in the project plan.
- list and describe each component of each subsidiary document that is included as a part of the project management plan.
- explain why it is necessary to have subsidiary documents included as a part of the project plan.
- explain why it is necessary to address all components of the planning process before deciding which processes are necessary to be completed based on the nature and scope of the project.
- explain why it is necessary to revisit one or more planning processes throughout the life of the project.

**AS YOU READ THIS CHAPTER, BE SURE THAT YOU UNDERSTAND THE FOLLOWING TERMS AND IDEAS.**

- Scope Plan
- Create WBS
- Activity Resource Estimating
- Cost Estimating
- Develop HR Plan
- Risk Identification
- Risk Response Plan

- Collect Requirements
- Activities Definition
- Activity Duration Estimating
- Determine Budget
- Plan Communications
- Qualitative Risk Analysis
- Plan Procurement

- Scope Definition
- Activities Sequencing
- Schedule Development

- Quality Planning
- Risk Management Plan
- Quantitative Risk Analysis

## REQUIREMENTS TO COMPLETE SECTION

To successfully complete this section, you must
- complete the learning check
- complete the learning in action requirements
- complete the on-the-job activities, and
- answer brain teaser questions assigned by instructor.

## TIME REQUIRED

This section is included as a part of unit three. Three weeks is allotted for successful completion of unit three.

## SIGN-OFF

Sign off for this section will be completed by the instructor.

## RESOURCES

The following outlines the resources that you will need to complete this section

- PMBOK Guide fourth edition, sections 4.2, 5.1, 5.2, 5.3, 6.1, 6.2, 6.3, 6.4, 6.5, 7.1, 7.2, 8.1, 9.1, 10.2, 11.1, 11.2, 11.3, 11.4, 11.5, 12.1.
- Heldman, fifth edition chapters 3-7.

## INSTRUCTIONS

Follow the steps below to complete this section and learning check.

| Step | Action |
|------|--------|
| 1 | Read the material in this section including the pages indicated in the resources section above. |
| 2 | Write down any notes or questions that you may wish to discuss with your instructor during your scheduled class. |
| 3 | Discuss any questions and/or concerns with your instructor. |
| 4 | Complete the learning in action, brain teaser and/or on-the-job activities presented by the instructor. |

## PROJECT PLAN

Fill in the blanks with the correct descriptor

| Begin With | Project Charter |
|---|---|
| 1. Project Charter | _____<br>_____<br>_____ |
| 1. Outputs from Planning Processes | **Outputs from Planning Processes**<br>_____<br>_____<br>_____<br>_____<br>_____ |
| 2. Enterprise Environmental Factors | **Enterprise Environmental Factors**<br>_____<br>_____<br>_____ |
| 3. Organizational Process Assets | **Organizational Process Assets**<br>_____<br>_____<br>_____<br>_____ |
| **Method** | **Expert Judgment** |
| 1. Use Expert Judgment | _____<br>_____<br>_____ |
| **Result** | **Project Management Plan** |
| 1. Project Management Plan | _____<br>_____<br>_____ |

## COLLECT REQUIREMENTS

Fill in the blanks with the correct descriptor

| **Begin With** | **Project Charter** |
|---|---|
| 1. Project Charter | _____ <br> _____ <br> _____ |
| 2. Stakeholder Register | **Stakeholder Register** <br> _____ <br> _____ <br> _____ <br> _____ |
| **Method** | **Interviews** |
| 1. Use Interviews | _____ <br> _____ <br> _____ |
| 2. Focus Groups | **Focus Groups** <br> _____ <br> _____ |
| 3. Facilitated Workshops | **Facilitated Workshops** <br> _____ <br> _____ |
| 4. Group Creativity Techniques | **Group Creativity Techniques** <br> _____ <br> _____ |
| 5. Group Decision Making Techniques | **Group Decision Making Techniques** <br> _____ <br> _____ |
| 6. Questionnaires and Surveys | **Questionnaires and Surveys** <br> _____ <br> _____ <br> _____ |

## COLLECT REQUIREMENTS CONT.

Fill in the blanks with the correct descriptor

| | |
|---|---|
| 7. Observations | **Observations** <br> _____ <br> _____ <br> _____ <br> _____ |
| 8. Prototypes | **Prototypes** <br> _____ <br> _____ <br> _____ <br> _____ |
| **Result** <br><br> 1. Requirements Documentation <br><br><br> 2. Requirements Management Plan <br><br><br> 3. Requirements Traceability Matrix | **Requirements Documentation** <br> _____ <br> _____ <br> _____ <br><br> **Requirements Management Plan** <br> _____ <br> _____ <br> _____ <br><br> **Requirements Traceability Matrix** <br> _____ <br> _____ <br> _____ |

## SCOPE DEFINITION

Fill in the blanks with the correct descriptor

| Begin With | Project Charter |
|---|---|
| 1. Project Charter | _____ _____ _____ |
| 2. Requirements Documentation | **Requirements Documentation** _____ _____ _____ |
| 3. Organizational Process Assets | **Organizational Process Assets** _____ _____ _____ |
| **Method** | **Product Analysis** |
| 1. Use Product Analysis | _____ _____ _____ |
| 2. Alternatives Identification | **Alternatives Identification** _____ _____ _____ |
| 3. Expert Judgment | **Expert Judgment** _____ _____ _____ _____ |
| 4. Facilitated Workshops | **Facilitated Workshops** _____ _____ _____ |
| **Result** | **Project Scope Statement** |
| 1. Scope Statement | _____ _____ |
| 2. Project Documents Update | **Project Documents Update** _____ _____ _____ _____ |

## CREATE WORK BREAKDOWN STRUCTURE (WBS)

Fill in the blanks with the correct descriptor

| Begin With | Project Scope Statement |
|---|---|
| 1. Project Scope Statement | |
| 2. Organizational Process Assets | **Organizational Process Assets** |
| 3. Requirements Documentation | **Requirements Documentation** |
| **Method** | **Decomposition** |
| 1. Use Decomposition | |
| **Result** | **Work Breakdown Structure** |
| 1. Work Breakdown Structure | |
| 2. Work Breakdown Structure Dictionary | **Work Breakdown Structure Dictionary** |
| 3. Scope Baseline | **Scope Baseline** |
| 4. Updates to the Project Documents | **Updates to the Project Documents** |

## ACTIVITY DEFINITION

Fill in the blanks with the correct descriptor

| Begin With | Enterprise Environmental Factors |
|---|---|
| 1. Enterprise Environmental Factors | _____ |
| | **Organizational Process Assets** |
| 2. Organizational Process Assets | _____ |
| 3. Scope Baseline | **Scope Baseline** |
| | _____ |
| **Method** | **Expert Judgment** |
| 1. Use Expert Judgment | _____ |
| 2. Decomposition | **Decomposition** |
| | _____ |
| 3. Templates | **Templates** |
| | _____ |
| 4. Rolling Wave Planning | **Rolling Wave Planning** |
| | _____ |

## ACTIVITY DEFINITION CONT.

Fill in the blanks with the correct descriptor

| Result | |
|---|---|
| **Result**<br><br>1. Activity Lists<br><br><br><br>2. Activity Attributes<br><br><br><br>3. Milestone Lists | **Activity Lists**<br>_____<br>_____<br>_____<br><br>**Activity Attributes**<br>_____<br>_____<br>_____<br><br>**Milestone Lists**<br>_____<br>_____<br>_____ |

## ACTIVITY SEQUENCING

Fill in the blanks with the correct descriptor

| **Begin With** | **Project Scope Statement** |
|---|---|
| 1. Project Scope Statement | _____ _____ _____ |
| 2. Activity Lists | **Activity Lists** _____ _____ _____ |
| 3. Activity Attributes | **Activity Attributes** _____ _____ _____ |
| 4. Milestone Lists | **Milestone Lists** _____ _____ _____ |
| 5. Organizational Process Assets | **Organizational Process Assets** _____ _____ _____ |

## ACTIVITY SEQUENCING CONT.

Fill in the blanks with the correct descriptor

| **Method** | **Precedence Diagramming Method** |
|---|---|
| 1. Use Precedence Diagramming Method | _____<br>_____<br>_____ |
| 2. Schedule Network Template | **Schedule Network Template**<br>_____<br>_____<br>_____ |
| 3. Dependency Determination | **Dependency Determination**<br>_____<br>_____<br>_____ |
| 4. Applying Lags and Leads | **Applying Leads and Lags**<br>_____<br>_____<br>_____ |
| **Result** | **Project Schedule Network Diagram** |
| 1. Project Schedule Network Diagram | _____<br>_____<br>_____ |
| 2. Project Document Updates | **Project Document Updates**<br>_____<br>_____<br>_____ |

## ACTIVITY RESOURCE ESTIMATING

Fill in the blanks with the correct descriptor

| **Begin With** | **Enterprise Environmental Factors** |
|---|---|
| 1. Enterprise Environmental Factors | _____ _____ _____ |
| 2. Organizational Process Assets | **Organizational Process Assets** _____ _____ _____ |
| 3. Activity Lists | **Activity Lists** _____ _____ _____ |
| 4. Activity Attributes | **Activity Attributes** _____ _____ _____ |
| 5. Resource Availability | **Resource Availability** _____ _____ _____ |
| 6. Resource Calendars | **Resource Calendars** _____ _____ _____ |

## ACTIVITY RESOURCE ESTIMATING CONT.

Fill in the blanks with the correct descriptor

| Method | Expert Judgment |
|---|---|
| 1. Use Expert Judgment | _____ |
| | **Alternatives Analysis** |
| 2. Alternatives Analysis | _____ |
| 3. Published Estimating Data | **Published Estimating Data** |
| | _____ |
| 4. Project Management Software | **Project Management Software** |
| | _____ |
| 5. Bottom up Estimating | **Bottom up Estimating** |
| | _____ |
| **Result** | **Activity Resource Requirements** |
| 1. Activity Resource Requirements | _____ |
| 2. Resource Breakdown Structure | **Resource Breakdown Structure** |
| | _____ |
| 3. Project Document Updates | **Project Document Updates** |
| | _____ |

## ACTIVITY DURATION ESTIMATING

Fill in the blanks with the correct descriptor

| Begin With | |
|---|---|
| **1.** Enterprise Environmental Factors | **Enterprise Environmental Factors** _____ _____ _____ |
| **2.** Organizational Process Assets | **Organizational Process Assets** _____ _____ _____ |
| **3.** Project Scope Statement | **Project Scope Statement** _____ _____ _____ |
| **4.** Activity List | **Activity List** _____ _____ _____ |
| **5.** Activity Attributes | **Activity Attributes** _____ _____ _____ |
| **6.** Activity Resource Requirements | **Activity Resource Requirements** _____ _____ _____ |
| **7.** Resource Calendar | **Resource Calendar** _____ _____ _____ |

## ACTIVITY DURATION ESTIMATING CONT.

Fill in the blanks with the correct descriptor

| Method | |
|---|---|
| | **Expert Judgment** |
| 1. Use Expert Judgment | _____ |
| | _____ |
| | _____ |
| | |
| 2. Analogous Estimating | **Analogous Estimating** |
| | _____ |
| | _____ |
| | |
| | **Parametric Estimating** |
| | _____ |
| 3. Parametric Estimating | _____ |
| | _____ |
| | |
| | **Three Point Estimates** |
| 4. Three Point Estimates | _____ |
| | _____ |
| | _____ |
| | |
| | **Reserve Analysis** |
| 5. Reserve Analysis | _____ |
| | _____ |
| | _____ |
| **Result** | |
| | **Activity Duration Estimates** |
| 1. Activity Duration Estimates | _____ |
| | _____ |
| | _____ |
| | |
| 2. Project Document Updates | **Project Document Updates** |
| | _____ |
| | _____ |
| | _____ |

## SCHEDULE DEVELOPMENT

Fill in the blanks with the correct descriptor

| **Begin With** | **Enterprise Environmental Factors** |
|---|---|
| 1. Enterprise Environmental Factors | _____ _____ _____ |
| 2. Organizational Process Assets | **Organizational Process Assets** _____ _____ _____ |
| 3. Project Scope Statement | **Project Scope Statement** _____ _____ _____ |
| 4. Activity List | **Activity List** _____ _____ _____ |
| 5. Activity Attributes | **Activity Attributes** _____ _____ _____ |
| 6. Project Schedule Network Diagrams | **Project Schedule Network Diagrams** _____ _____ _____ |
| 7. Activity Resource Requirements | **Activity Resource Requirements** _____ _____ _____ |
| 8. Resource Calendars | **Resource Calendars** _____ _____ _____ |
| 9. Activity Duration Estimates | **Activity Duration Estimates** _____ _____ _____ |

## SCHEDULE DEVELOPMENT CONT.

Fill in the blanks with the correct descriptor

| Method | |
|---|---|
| 1. Use Schedule Network Analysis | **Schedule Network Analysis** |
| 2. Critical Path Method | **Critical Path Method** |
| 3. Schedule Compression | **Schedule Compression** |
| 4. What-if Scenario Analysis | **What-if Scenario Analysis** |
| 5. Resource Leveling | **Resource Leveling** |
| 6. Critical Chain Method | **Critical Chain Method** |
| 7. Applying Leads and Lags | **Applying Leads and Lags** |
| 8. Scheduling Tool | **Scheduling Tool** |

## SCHEDULE DEVELOPMENT CONT.

Fill in the blanks with the correct descriptor

| Result | |
|---|---|
| **Result** | **Project Schedule** <br> _____ <br> _____ <br> _____ |
| 1. Project Schedule | |
| 2. Schedule Data | **Schedule Data** <br> _____ <br> _____ <br> _____ |
| 3. Schedule Baseline | **Schedule Baseline** <br> _____ <br> _____ <br> _____ |
| 4. Project Document Updates | **Project Document Updates** <br> _____ <br> _____ <br> _____ |

## COST ESTIMATING

Fill in the blanks with the correct descriptor

| Begin With | Enterprise Environmental Factors |
|---|---|
| 1. Enterprise Environmental Factors | _____ _____ _____ |
| 2. Organizational Process Assets | **Organizational Process Assets** _____ _____ _____ |
| 3. Scope Baseline | **Scope Baseline** _____ _____ _____ |
| 4. Project Schedule | **Project Schedule** _____ _____ _____ |
| 5. Human Resources Plan | **Human Resources Plan** _____ _____ _____ |
| 6. Risk Register | **Risk Register** _____ _____ _____ |

## COST ESTIMATING CONT.

Fill in the blanks with the correct descriptor

| Method | Expert Judgment |
|---|---|
| 1. Use Expert Judgment | _____<br>_____ |
| 2. Analogous Estimating | **Analogous Estimating**<br>_____<br>_____ |
| 3. Bottom Up Estimating | **Bottom Up Estimating**<br>_____<br>_____ |
| 4. Parametric Estimating | **Parametric Estimating**<br>_____<br>_____ |
| 5. Project Management Software | **Project Management Software**<br>_____<br>_____ |
| 6. Vendor Bid Analysis | **Vendor Bid Analysis**<br>_____<br>_____ |
| 7. Reserve Analysis | **Reserve Analysis**<br>_____<br>_____ |
| 8. Cost of Quality | **Cost of Quality**<br>_____<br>_____ |
| 9. Three Point Estimates | **Three Point Estimates**<br>_____<br>_____ |

## COST ESTIMATING CONT.

Fill in the blanks with the correct descriptor

| Result | Activity Cost Estimates and Supporting Detail |
|---|---|
| 1. Activity Cost Estimates and Supporting Detail | _____<br>_____<br>_____ |
| 2. Basis of Estimates | **Basis of Estimates**<br>_____<br>_____<br>_____ |
| 3. Project Document Updates | **Project Document Updates**<br>_____<br>_____<br>_____ |

## COST BUDGETING

Fill in the blanks with the correct descriptor

| **Begin With** | **Organizational Process Assets** |
|---|---|
| 1. Organizational Process Assets | _____<br>_____<br>_____ |
| 2. Project Scope Statement | **Project Scope Statement**<br>_____<br>_____<br>_____ |
| 3. Activity Cost Estimate and Supporting Detail | **Activity Cost Estimate and Supporting Detail**<br>_____<br>_____<br>_____ |
| 4. Project Schedule | **Project Schedule**<br>_____<br>_____<br>_____ |
| 5. Resource Calendars | **Resource Calendars**<br>_____<br>_____<br>_____ |
| 6. Contract | **Contract**<br>_____<br>_____<br>_____ |
| 7. Basis of Estimates | **Basis of Estimates**<br>_____<br>_____<br>_____ |

## COST BUDGETING CONT.

Fill in the blanks with the correct descriptor

| Method | |
|---|---|
| | **Expert Judgment** <br> _____ <br> _____ <br> _____ |
| 1. Use Expert Judgment | |
| 2. Cost Aggregation | **Cost Aggregation** <br> _____ <br> _____ <br> _____ |
| 3. Reserve Analysis | **Reserve Analysis** <br> _____ <br> _____ <br> _____ |
| 4. Funding Limit Reconciliation | **Funding Limit Reconciliation** <br> _____ <br> _____ |
| 5. Historical Relationships | **Historical Relationships** <br> _____ <br> _____ <br> _____ <br> _____ |
| **Result** | |
| | **Cost Baseline** <br> _____ <br> _____ <br> _____ |
| 1. Cost Baseline | |
| 2. Project Funding Requirements | **Project Funding Requirements** <br> _____ <br> _____ |
| 3. Project Document Updates | **Project Document Updates** <br> _____ <br> _____ <br> _____ |

## QUALITY PLANNING

Fill in the blanks with the correct descriptor

| **Begin With** | **Enterprise Environmental Factors** |
|---|---|
| 1. Enterprise Environmental Factors | _____<br>_____<br>_____ |
| 2. Organizational Process Assets | **Organizational Process Assets**<br>_____<br>_____<br>_____ |
| 3. Project Scope Baseline | **Project Scope Baseline**<br>_____<br>_____<br>_____ |
| 4. Stakeholder Register | **Stakeholder Register**<br>_____<br>_____<br>_____ |
| 5. Cost Baseline | **Cost Baseline**<br>_____<br>_____<br>_____ |
| 6. Schedule Baseline | **Schedule Baseline**<br>_____<br>_____<br>_____ |
| 7. Risk Register | **Risk Register**<br>_____<br>_____<br>_____ |

## QUALITY PLANNING CONT.

Fill in the blanks with the correct descriptor

| Method | |
|---|---|
| **Method** | **Cost Benefit Analysis** |
| 1. Cost Benefit Analysis | _____ |
| 2. Benchmarking | **Benchmarking** _____ |
| 3. Design of Experiments | **Design of Experiments** _____ |
| 4. Cost of Quality | **Cost of Quality** _____ |
| 5. Additional Quality Planning Tools | **Additional Quality Planning Tools** _____ |
| 6. Control Charts | **Control Charts** _____ |
| 7. Statistical Sampling | **Statistical Sampling** _____ |
| 8. Flowcharting | **Flowcharting** _____ |
| 9. Proprietary Quality Management Methodologies | **Proprietary Quality Management Methodologies** _____ |

## QUALITY PLANNING CONT.

Fill in the blanks with the correct descriptor

| Result | |
|---|---|
| **1.** Quality Management Plan | **Quality Management Plan** <br> _____ <br> _____ <br> _____ |
| **2.** Quality Metrics | **Quality Metrics** <br> _____ <br> _____ <br> _____ |
| **3.** Quality Checklists | **Quality Checklists** <br> _____ <br> _____ <br> _____ |
| **4.** Process Improvement Plan | **Process Improvement Plan** <br> _____ <br> _____ <br> _____ |
| **5.** Project Document Updates | **Project Document Updates** <br> _____ <br> _____ <br> _____ |

## HUMAN RESOURCES MANAGEMENT PLAN

Fill in the blanks with the correct descriptor

| Begin With | Enterprise Environmental Factors |
|---|---|
| 1. Enterprise Environmental Factors | |
| 2. Organizational Process Assets | **Organizational Process Assets** |
| 3. Activity Resource Requirements | **Activity Resource Requirements** |

| Method | Organization Charts and Position Descriptions |
|---|---|
| 1. Use Organization Charts and Position Descriptions | |
| 2. Networking | **Networking** |
| 3. Organizational Theory | **Organizational Theory** |

## HUMAN RESOURCES MANAGEMENT PLAN CONT.

Fill in the blanks with the correct descriptor

| Result | The Human Resources Plan |
|---|---|
| 1. Human Resources Plan | _____<br>_____<br>_____ |

## COMMUNICATION PLANNING

Fill in the blanks with the correct descriptor

| Begin With | Enterprise Environmental Factors |
|---|---|
| 1. Enterprise Environmental Factors | _____ _____ _____ |
| 2. Organizational Process Assets | **Organizational Process Assets** _____ _____ _____ |
| 3. Project Charter | **Project Charter** _____ _____ _____ _____ |
| 4. Procurement Documents | **Procurement Documents** _____ _____ _____ _____ |
| **Method** | **Expert Judgment** |
| 1. Use Expert Judgment | _____ _____ _____ |
| 2. Stakeholder Analysis | **Stakeholder Analysis** _____ _____ _____ |
| **Result** | **Stakeholder Register** |
| 1. Stakeholder Register | _____ _____ _____ |
| 2. Stakeholder Management Strategy | **Stakeholder Management Strategy** _____ _____ _____ |

## RISK MANAGEMENT PLAN

Fill in the blanks with the correct descriptor

| **Begin With** | **Enterprise Environmental Factors** |
|---|---|
| 1. Enterprise Environmental Factors | _____ <br> _____ <br> _____ |
| 2. Organizational Process Assets | **Organizational Process Assets** <br> _____ <br> _____ <br> _____ |
| 3. Project Scope Statement | **Project Scope Statement** <br> _____ <br> _____ <br> _____ |
| 4. Cost Management Plan | **Cost Management Plan** <br> _____ <br> _____ <br> _____ |
| 5. Schedule Management Plan | **Schedule Management Plan** <br> _____ <br> _____ <br> _____ |
| 6. Communications Management Plan | **Communications Management Plan** <br> _____ <br> _____ <br> _____ |

## RISK MANAGEMENT PLAN CONT.

Fill in the blanks with the correct descriptor

| Method | Planning Meetings and Analysis |
|---|---|
| 1. Planning Meetings and Analysis | _____<br>_____<br>_____<br>_____<br>_____<br>_____<br>_____<br>_____<br>_____ |
| **Result** | **Risk Management Plan** |
| 1. Risk Management Plan | _____<br>_____<br>_____<br>_____<br>_____<br>_____ |

## RISK IDENTIFICATION

Fill in the blanks with the correct descriptor

| Begin With | |
|---|---|
| **Begin With** | **Enterprise Environmental Factors** <br> _____ <br> _____ <br> _____ |
| 1. Enterprise Environmental Factors | |
| 2. Organizational Process Assets | **Organizational Process Assets** <br> _____ <br> _____ <br> _____ |
| 3. Scope Baseline | **Scope Baseline** <br> _____ <br> _____ <br> _____ |
| 4. Risk Management Plan | **Risk Management Plan** <br> _____ <br> _____ <br> _____ |
| 5. Activity Cost Estimates | **Activity Cost Estimates and Supporting Detail** <br> _____ <br> _____ <br> _____ <br> _____ <br> _____ <br> _____ <br> _____ |
| 6. Activity Duration Estimates | **Activity Duration Estimates** <br> _____ <br> _____ <br> _____ |
| 7. Stakeholder Register | **Stakeholder Register** <br> _____ <br> _____ <br> _____ |

## RISK IDENTIFICATION CONT.

Fill in the blanks with the correct descriptor

| Begin With | Cost Management Plan |
|---|---|
| 8. Cost Management Plan | _____ <br> _____ <br> _____ |
| 9. Schedule Management Plan | **Schedule Management Plan** <br> _____ <br> _____ <br> _____ |
| 10. Quality Management Plan | **Quality Management Plan** <br> _____ <br> _____ <br> _____ |
| 11. Project Documents | **Project Documents** <br> _____ <br> _____ <br> _____ <br> _____ |

## RISK IDENTIFICATION CONT.

Fill in the blanks with the correct descriptor

| **Method** | **Documentation Reviews** |
|---|---|
| 1. Use Documentation Reviews | _____ _____ _____ |
| 2. Information Gathering Techniques | **Information Gathering Techniques** _____ _____ _____ |
| 3. Checklist Analysis | **Checklist Analysis** _____ _____ _____ |
| 4. Assumptions Analysis | **Assumptions Analysis** _____ _____ _____ _____ _____ _____ |
| 5. Diagramming Techniques | **Diagramming Techniques** _____ _____ _____ _____ _____ _____ _____ _____ _____ |

## RISK IDENTIFICATION CONT.

Fill in the blank with the correct descriptor

| **Method** | **Expert Judgment** |
|---|---|
| 6. Expert Judgment | _____<br>_____<br>_____ |
| 7. SWOT Analysis | **SWOT Analysis**<br>_____<br>_____<br>_____<br>_____ |
| **Result** | _____<br>_____<br>_____ |
| 1. Risk Register | _____<br>_____<br>_____<br>_____ |

## QUALITATIVE RISK ANALYSIS

Fill in the blanks with the correct descriptor

| **Begin With** | **Organizational Process Assets** |
|---|---|
| 1. Organizational Process Assets | _____ _____ |
| 2. Project Scope Statement | **Project Scope Statement** _____ _____ |
| 3. Risk Management Plan | **Risk Management Plan** _____ _____ |
| 4. Risk Register | **Risk Register** _____ _____ _____ |
| **Method** | **Risk Probability and Impact Assessment** |
| 1. Use Risk Probability and Impact Assessment | _____ _____ _____ |
| 2. Probability and Impact Matrix | **Probability and Impact Matrix** _____ _____ |
| 3. Risk Categorization | **Risk Categorization** _____ _____ |
| 4. Risk Data Quality Assessment | **Risk Data Quality Assessment** _____ _____ |
| 5. Risk Urgency Assessment | **Risk Urgency Assessment** _____ _____ |
| 6. Expert Judgment | **Expert Judgment** _____ _____ |

## QUALITATIVE RISK ANALYSIS CONT

Fill in the blanks with the correct descriptor

| Result | Risk Register Updates |
|---|---|
| 1. Risk Register Updates | _____ <br> _____ <br> _____ <br> _____ <br> _____ <br> _____ |

## QUANTITATIVE RISK ANALYSIS

Fill in the blanks with the correct descriptor

| **Begin With** | **Organizational Process Assets** |
|---|---|
| 1. Organizational Process Assets | \
\
\
\
\
\
\ |
| 2. Risk Management Plan | **Risk Management Plan**<br>\
\
\
\
\
\ |
| 3. Risk Register | **Risk Register**<br>\
\
\
\
\
\
\ |
| 4. Cost Management Plan | **Cost Management Plan**<br>\
\
\
\
\
\ |
| 5. Schedule Management Plan | **Schedule Management Plan**<br>\
\
\
\
\
\
\ |

## QUANTITATIVE RISK ANALYSIS CONT.

Fill in the blanks with the correct descriptor

| Method | Expert Judgment |
|---|---|
| 1. Use Expert Judgment | _____ |
| | _____ |
| | _____ |
| 2. Data Gathering and Representation Techniques | **Data Gathering and Representation Techniques** |
| | _____ |
| | _____ |
| | _____ |
| 3. Quantitative Risk Analysis and Modeling Techniques | **Quantitative Risk Analysis and Modeling Techniques** |
| | _____ |
| | _____ |
| | _____ |
| | _____ |
| | _____ |
| | _____ |
| | _____ |
| **Result** | **Risk Register Updates** |
| 1. Risk Register Updates | _____ |
| | _____ |
| | _____ |

## RISK RESPONSE PLANNING

Fill in the blanks with the correct descriptor

| Begin With | Risk Management Plan |
|---|---|
| 1. Risk Management Plan | _____ |
| 2. Risk Register | **Risk Register** _____ |
| **Method** | **Strategies for Negative Risks or Threats** |
| 1. Use Strategies for Negative Risks or Threats | _____ |
| 2. Strategies for Positive Risks or Opportunities | **Strategies for Positive Risks or Opportunities** _____ |
| 3. Contingent Response Strategy | **Contingent Response Strategy** _____ |
| 4. Expert Judgment | **Expert Judgment** _____ |

## RISK RESPONSE PLANNING CONT.

Fill in the blanks with the correct descriptor

| Result | |
|---|---|
| | **Updates to Risk Register** |
| 1. Updates to Risk Register | |
| 2. Risk Related Contractual Agreements | **Risk Related Contractual Agreements** |
| 3. Updates to Project Management Plan | **Updates to Project Management Plan** |
| 4. Project Document Updates | **Project Document Updates** |

## PLAN PROCUREMENTS

Fill in the blanks with the correct descriptor

| **Begin With** | |
| --- | --- |
| 1. Enterprise Environmental Factors | **Enterprise Environmental Factors** |
| 2. Organizational Process Assets | **Organizational Process Assets** |
| 3. Scope Baseline | **Scope Baseline** |
| 4. Requirements Documentation | **Requirements Documentation** |
| 5. Teaming Agreements | **Teaming Agreements** |
| 6. Risk Register | **Risk Register** |
| 7. Risk Related Contract Decisions | **Risk Related Contractual Decisions** |

## PLAN PROCUREMENTS CONT.

Fill in the blanks with the correct descriptor

| **Begin With** | **Activity Resource Requirements** |
|---|---|
| 8. Activity Resources Requirements | |
| 9. Project Schedule | **Project Schedule** |
| 10. Activity Cost Estimates | **Activity Cost Estimates and Supporting Detail** |
| 11. Cost Performance Baseline | **Cost Performance Baseline** |

## PLAN PROCUREMENTS CONT.

Fill in the blanks with the correct descriptor

| Method | Make or Buy Analysis |
|---|---|
| 1. Use Make or Buy Analysis | _____<br>_____<br>_____<br>_____<br>_____<br>_____ |
| 2. Contract Types | **Contract Types**<br>_____<br>_____<br>_____<br>_____<br>_____<br>_____<br>_____<br>_____ |
| 3. Expert Judgment | **Expert Judgment**<br>_____<br>_____<br>_____<br>_____<br>_____<br>_____ |

## PLAN PROCUREMENTS CONT.

Fill in the blanks with the correct descriptor

| Result | |
|---|---|
| **Procurement Management Plan** | |
| 1. Procurement Management Plan | _____ _____ _____ |
| 2. Procurement Statement of Work | **Procurement Statement of Work** _____ _____ _____ |
| 3. Make or Buy Decisions | **Make or Buy Decisions** _____ _____ _____ |
| 4. Requested Changes | **Requested Changes** _____ _____ _____ |
| 5. Procurement Documents | **Procurement Documents** _____ _____ _____ _____ _____ _____ |
| 6. Source Selection Criteria | **Source Selection Criteria** _____ _____ _____ _____ _____ |

**Explain the purpose of the project management plan**

_____
_____
_____
_____
_____

**List the subsidiary documents that are included in the project plan**

_____
_____
_____
_____
_____
_____
_____
_____
_____
_____
_____
_____
_____
_____
_____
_____
_____
_____
_____
_____
_____
_____
_____

**and Describe each component of each subsidiary document that is included as a part of the project management plan**

_____

_____

_____

_____

_____

**Explain why it is necessary to have subsidiary documents included as a part of the project Plan**

_____

_____

_____

_____

_____

**Explain why it is necessary to revisit one or more planning processes throughout the life of the project**

_____

_____

_____

_____

_____

**Explain why is it Necessary to Revisit One or More Planning Processes Throughout the Life of the Project**

_____

_____

_____

_____

_____

## LEARNING IN ACTION AND/OR ON-THE-JOB ACTIVITIES

The following is an activity that may be completed individually or as a small group. This activity is intended to assess your comprehension and application of the material that was previously covered. Answer the questions below and make some notes in the space provided.

Consider what happened on the last project that you were involved in or managed.

What factors contributed to the success of the project?

_____

_____

_____

_____

_____

Which of the factors contributing to the success of the project relate to the concepts covered in this section?

_____

_____

_____

_____

_____

What tasks that relate to the material previously covered, helped you to successfully complete your project?

_____

_____

_____

_____

List and describe the areas of the project where you experienced challenges?

_____

_____

_____

_____

What factors contributed to this?

_____

_____

_____

_____

_____

Given what you learned about the areas covered in the previous section, what would you do differently in your next project?

_____

_____

_____

_____

_____

What tasks did you neglect that may have contributed to a more successful outcome?

_____

_____

_____

_____

_____

## THINGS THAT I NEED TO WORK ON

The following are things that I need to work on to be proficient in the concepts covered in this chapter.

_____

_____

_____

_____

_____

_____

_____

_____

_____

_____

# PROJECT EXECUTION

**AFTER STUDYING THIS CHAPTER, YOU SHOULD BE ABLE TO**

- define project execution and explain its importance.
- list and describe the multiple actions required to be completed as a part of project execution.
- explain the purpose of quality assurance and describe what quality assurance entails.
- describe why it is necessary to use a formal process to acquire the project team. Explain how team members may be acquired and describe what this process entails.
- explain what developing the project team entails, explain why it is important to develop the team, and state who is responsible for project team development.
- explain why distributing project information is important, how is it done and how the lessons-learned activity fits into the overall process.
- describe the process for selecting sellers and explain some of the ways that the organization can ensure that sellers who are suitably qualified to perform the work of the project are selected.
- explain what activities take place as a part of directing and managing project execution.
- list and describe the project execution outputs.

**AS YOU READ THIS CHAPTER, BE SURE THAT YOU UNDERSTAND THE FOLLOWING TERMS AND IDEAS.**

- Direct and Manage Project Execution
- Perform Quality Assurance
- Acquire Project Team

- Develop Project Team
- Manage Project Team
- Distribute Information

- Manage Stakeholder Expectations
- Conduct Procurements

## REQUIREMENTS TO COMPLETE SECTION

To successfully complete this section, you must
- complete the learning check
- complete the learning in action requirements
- complete the on-the-job activities, and
- answer brain teaser questions assigned by instructor.

## TIME REQUIRED

This section is included as a part of unit four. Three weeks is allotted for successful completion of unit four.

## SIGN-OFF

Sign off for this section will be completed by the instructor.

## RESOURCES

The following outlines the resources that you will need to complete this section
- PMBOK Guide fourth edition, sections 4.3,8.2,9.2,9.3,9.4,10.3,10.4,12.2.
- Heldman, fifth edition chapter 8.

## INSTRUCTIONS

Follow the steps below to complete this section and learning check.

| Step | Action |
|------|--------|
| 1 | Read the material in this section including the pages indicated in the resources section above. |
| 2 | Write down any notes or questions that you may wish to discuss with your instructor during your scheduled class. |
| 3 | Discuss any questions and/or concerns with your instructor. |
| 4 | Complete the learning in action, brain teaser and/or on-the-job activities presented by the instructor. |

## DIRECT AND MANAGE PROJECT EXECUTION

Fill in the blanks with the correct descriptor

| **Begin With** | **Enterprise Environmental Factors** |
|---|---|
| 1. Enterprise Environmental Factors | |
| | **Organizational Process Assets** |
| 2. Organizational Process Assets | |
| 3. Project Management Plan | **Project Management Plan** |
| 4. Approved Change Requests | **Approved Change Requests** |
| **Method** | **Expert Judgment** |
| 1. Use Expert Judgment | |
| 2. Project Management Information System | **Project Management Information System** |

## DIRECT AND MANAGE PROJECT EXECUTION CONT.

Fill in the blanks with the correct descriptor

| **Result** | **Deliverables** |
|---|---|
| 1. Deliverables | _____<br>_____<br>_____<br>_____ |
| 2. Work Performance Information | **Work Performance Information**<br>_____<br>_____<br>_____<br>_____ |
| 3. Change Requests | **Change Requests**<br>_____<br>_____<br>_____ |
| 4. Project Management Plan Updates | **Project Management Plan Updates**<br>_____<br>_____<br>_____<br>_____ |
| 5. Project Document Updates | **Project Document Updates**<br>_____<br>_____<br>_____<br>_____ |

## PERFORM QUALITY ASSURANCE

Fill in the blanks with the correct descriptor

| Begin With | |
|---|---|
| | **Project Management Plan** |
| 1. Project Management Plan | _____ |
| | _____ |
| | _____ |
| 2. Quality Metrics | **Quality Metrics** |
| | _____ |
| | _____ |
| | _____ |
| 3. Work Performance Information | **Work Performance Information** |
| | _____ |
| | _____ |
| | _____ |
| 4. Quality Control Measures | **Quality Control Measures** |
| | _____ |
| | _____ |
| | _____ |
| | _____ |
| **Method** | **Plan Quality and Perform Quality Control Tools and Techniques** |
| 1. Plan Quality and Perform Quality Control | _____ |
| | _____ |
| | _____ |
| 2. Quality Audits | **Quality Audits** |
| | _____ |
| | _____ |
| | _____ |
| 3. Process Analysis | **Process Analysis** |
| | _____ |
| | _____ |
| | _____ |
| | _____ |

## PERFORM QUALITY ASSURANCE CONT.

Fill in the blanks with the correct descriptor

| Result | |
|---|---|
| **1.** Organizational Process Assets Updates<br><br>**2.** Change Requests<br><br>**3.** Project Management Plan Updates<br><br>**4.** Project Document Updates | **Organizational Process Assets Updates**<br>_____<br>_____<br>_____<br><br>**Change Requests**<br>_____<br>_____<br>_____<br><br>**Project Management Plan Updates**<br>_____<br>_____<br>_____<br><br>**Project Document Updates**<br>_____<br>_____<br>_____ |

## ACQUIRE THE PROJECT TEAM

Fill in the blanks with the correct descriptor

| Begin With | Enterprise Environmental Factors |
|---|---|
| 1. Enterprise Environmental Factors | _____ |
| | _____ |
| | _____ |
| 2. Organizational Process Assets | **Organizational Process Assets** |
| | _____ |
| | _____ |
| | _____ |
| 3. Project Management Plan | **Project Management Plan** |
| | _____ |
| | _____ |
| **Method** | **Pre-Assignment** |
| 1. Use Pre-Assignment | _____ |
| | _____ |
| | _____ |
| | _____ |
| 2. Negotiation | **Negotiation** |
| | _____ |
| | _____ |
| | _____ |
| | _____ |
| 3. Acquisition | **Acquisition** |
| | _____ |
| | _____ |
| | _____ |
| | _____ |
| 4. Virtual Teams | **Virtual Teams** |
| | _____ |
| | _____ |
| | _____ |
| | _____ |
| | _____ |
| | _____ |

## ACQUIRE THE PROJECT TEAM CONT.

Fill in the blanks with the correct descriptor

| Result | |
|---|---|
| **Project Staff Assignments** | |
| 1. Project Staff Assignments | _____ <br> _____ <br> _____ |
| 2. Resource Calendars | **Resource Calendars** <br> _____ <br> _____ <br> _____ |
| 3. Project Management Plan Updates | **Project Management Plan Updates** <br> _____ <br> _____ <br> _____ |

## DEVELOP THE PROJECT TEAM

Fill in the blanks with the correct descriptor

| Begin With | Project Staff Assignments |
|---|---|
| 1. Project Staff Assignments | _____ _____ _____ |
| 2. Project Management Plan | **Project Management Plan** _____ _____ _____ |
| 3. Resource Calendars | **Resource Calendars** _____ _____ _____ _____ |
| **Method** | **Interpersonal Skill** |
| 1. Use Interpersonal Skill | _____ _____ _____ |
| 2. Training | **Training** _____ _____ _____ |
| 3. Team Building Activities | **Team Building** _____ _____ _____ |
| 4. Ground Rules | **Ground Rules** _____ _____ _____ _____ _____ _____ |

## DEVELOP THE PROJECT TEAM CONT.

Fill in the blanks with the correct descriptor

| Method | Co-location |
|---|---|
| 5. Co-location | |
| | _____ |
| | _____ |
| | _____ |
| 6. Recognition and Rewards | **Recognition and Rewards** |
| | _____ |
| | _____ |
| | _____ |
| **Result** | **Team Performance Assessments** |
| 1. Team Performance Assessments | _____ |
| | _____ |
| | _____ |
| 2. Enterprise Environmental Factors Updates | **Enterprise Environmental Factors Updates** |
| | _____ |
| | _____ |
| | _____ |

## DISTRIBUTE PROJECT INFORMATION

Fill in the blanks with the correct descriptor

| Begin With | Organizational Process Assets |
|---|---|
| 1. Organizational Process Assets | _____ _____ _____ |
| 2. Project Management Plan | **Project Management Plan** _____ _____ _____ _____ |
| 3. Performance Reports | **Performance Reports** _____ _____ _____ _____ _____ |
| **Method** | |
| 1. Use Communication Methods | **Communication Methods** _____ _____ _____ _____ |
| 2. Information Distribution Tools | **Information Distribution Tools** _____ _____ _____ _____ |
| **Result** | |
| 1. Organizational Process Assets Updates | **Organizational Process Assets Updates** _____ _____ _____ _____ _____ |

## MANAGE STAKEHOLDER EXPECTATIONS

Fill in the blanks with the correct descriptor

| **Begin With** | **Stakeholder Register** |
|---|---|
| | _____ |
| | _____ |
| 1.  Stakeholder Register | _____ |
| | **Stakeholder Management Strategy** |
| 2.  Stakeholder Management Strategy | _____ |
| | _____ |
| | _____ |
| 3.  Project Management Plan | **Project Management Plan** |
| | _____ |
| | _____ |
| | _____ |
| 4.  Issues Log | **Issues Log** |
| | _____ |
| | _____ |
| | _____ |
| 5.  Change Log | **Change Log** |
| | _____ |
| | _____ |
| | _____ |
| 6.  Organizational Process Assets | **Organizational Process Assets** |
| | _____ |
| | _____ |
| | _____ |
| | _____ |
| | _____ |

## MANAGE STAKEHOLDER EXPECTATIONS CONT.

Fill in the blanks with the correct descriptor

| Method | Communication Methods |
|---|---|
| 1. Use Communication Methods | _____<br>_____<br>_____<br>_____ |
| 2. Interpersonal Skills | **Interpersonal Skills**<br>_____<br>_____<br>_____ |
| 3. Management Skills | **Management Skills**<br>_____<br>_____<br>_____<br>_____ |
| **Result** | **Organizational Process Assets Updates** |
| 1. Organizational Process Assets Updates | _____<br>_____ |
| 2. Change Requests | **Change Requests**<br>_____<br>_____<br>_____ |
| 3. Project Management Plan Updates | **Project Management Plan Updates**<br>_____<br>_____<br>_____ |
| 4. Project Document Updates | **Project Document Updates**<br>_____<br>_____<br>_____<br>_____<br>_____ |

## CONDUCT PROCUREMENTS

Fill in the blanks with the correct descriptor

| **Begin With** | **Project Management Plan** |
|---|---|
| 1. Project Management Plan | |
| 2. Procurement Documents | **Procurement Documents** |
| 3. Source Selection Criteria | **Source Selection Criteria** |
| 4. Qualified Seller List | **Qualified Seller List** |
| 5. Seller Proposals | **Seller Proposals** |

## CONDUCT PROCUREMENTS CONT.

Fill in the blanks with the correct descriptor

| Begin With | Project Documents |
|---|---|
| 6. Project Documents | _____ <br> _____ <br> _____ |
| | **Make or Buy Decisions** |
| 7. Make or Buy Decisions | _____ <br> _____ <br> _____ <br> _____ <br> _____ <br> _____ <br> _____ <br> _____ |
| 8. Teaming Agreements | **Teaming Agreements** <br> _____ <br> _____ <br> _____ <br> _____ <br> _____ <br> _____ <br> _____ <br> _____ |
| 9. Organizational Process Assets | **Organizational Process Assets** <br> _____ <br> _____ <br> _____ <br> _____ <br> _____ |

## Conduct Procurements Cont.

Fill in the blanks with the correct descriptor

| Method | |
|---|---|
| 1. Use Bidder Conferences | **Use Bidder Conferences** |
| 2. Proposal Evaluations | **Proposal Evaluations** |
| 3. Independent Estimates | **Independent Estimates** |
| 4. Expert Judgment | **Expert Judgment** |
| 5. Advertising | **Advertising** |
| 6. Internet Search | **Internet Search** |
| 7. Procurement Negotiations | **Procurement Negotiations** |

## CONDUCT PROCUREMENTS CONT.

Fill in the blanks with the correct descriptor

| Result | |
|---|---|
| **Result** | **Selected Sellers** |
| 1. Selected Sellers | _____ |
| 2. Procurement Contract Award | **Procurement Contract Award** |
| 3. Resource Calendars | **Resource Calendars** |
| 4. Change Requests | **Change Requests** |
| 5. Project Management Plan Updates | **Project Management Plan Updates** |
| 6. Project Document Updates | **Project Document Updates** |

**Define project execution and explain its importance.**

_____

_____

_____

_____

_____

**List and describe the multiple actions required to be completed as a part of project execution.**

_____

_____

_____

_____

_____

**Explain the purpose of quality assurance and describe what quality assurance entails.**

_____

_____

_____

_____

_____

**Describe the process for selecting sellers and explain some of the ways that the organization can ensure that sellers who are suitably qualified to perform the work of the project are selected.**

_____

_____

_____

_____

_____

_____

_____

_____

_____

_____

**Describe why it is necessary to use a formal process to acquire the project team. Explain how team members may be acquired and describe what this process entails.**

_____

_____

_____

_____

_____

_____

_____

_____

_____

_____

**Explain what developing the project team entails, explain why it is important to develop the team, and state who is responsible for project team development.**

_____

_____

_____

_____

**Explain why distributing project information is important, how is it done and how the lessons-learned activity fits into the overall process.**

_____

_____

_____

**Explain what activities take place as a part of directing and managing project execution.**

_____

_____

_____

_____

_____

_____

**List and describe the project execution outputs.**

_____

_____

_____

_____

_____

_____

_____

_____

_____

## LEARNING IN ACTION AND/OR ON-THE-JOB ACTIVITIES

The following is an activity that may be completed individually or as a small group. This activity is intended to assess your comprehension and application of the material that was previously covered. Answer the questions below and make some notes in the space provided.

Consider what happened on the last project that you were involved in or managed.

What factors contributed to the success of the project?

_____

_____

_____

_____

_____

Which of the factors contributing to the success of the project relate to the concepts covered in this section?

_____

_____

_____

_____

_____

What tasks that relate to the material previously covered, helped you to successfully complete your project?

_____

_____

_____

_____

_____

List and describe the areas of the project where you experienced challenges?

_____

_____

_____

_____

_____

What factors contributed to this?

_____

_____

_____

_____

_____

Given what you learned about the areas covered in the previous section, what would you do differently in your next project?

_____

_____

_____

_____

_____

What tasks did you neglect that may have contributed to a more successful outcome?

_____

_____

_____

_____

_____

## THINGS THAT I NEED TO WORK ON

The following are things that I need to work on to be proficient in the concepts covered in this chapter.

_____

_____

_____

_____

_____

_____

_____

_____

_____

# MONITORING AND CONTROLLING THE PROJECT

- explain the purpose of monitoring and controlling the project
- describe the activities that take place in monitoring and controlling the project plan.
- explain the purpose of integrated change control and describe the activities that take place in this area.
- explain the purpose of scope verification and scope control and describe what takes place in each of these areas.
- explain why monitoring and controlling the project schedule is important.
- explain why it is important to monitor and control cost in a project.
- state the purpose of performing quality control when monitoring and controlling the project.
- list the types of documents that may be needed to monitor and control the work of the project team.
- list and describe the type of documents that are produced for performance reporting as a part of managing and controlling the project plan.
- state the importance of managing communications to stakeholders.
- explain the activities that take place as a part of risk monitoring and controlling.
- explain the activities that take place as a part of contract administration.

**AS YOU READ THIS CHAPTER, BE SURE THAT YOU UNDERSTAND THE FOLLOWING TERMS AND IDEAS.**

- Monitor and Control Project Work
- Control Schedule
- Report Performance

- Perform Integrated Change Control
- Control Costs
- Monitor and Control Risks

- Verify Scope
- Control Scope
- Perform Quality Control
- Administer Procurements

## REQUIREMENTS TO COMPLETE SECTION

To successfully complete this section, you must
- complete the learning check
- complete the learning in action requirements
- complete the on-the-job activities, and
- answer brain teaser questions assigned by instructor.

## TIME REQUIRED

This section is included as a part of unit five. Three weeks is allotted for successful completion of unit five.

## SIGN-OFF

Sign off for this section will be completed by the instructor.

## RESOURCES

The following outlines the resources that you will need to complete this section
- PMBOK Guide fourth edition, sections 4.4, 4.5, 5.4, 5.5, 6.6, 7.3, 8.3, 10.5, 11.6, 12.3.
- Heldman, fifth edition chapters 9, 10 and 11.

## INSTRUCTIONS

Follow the steps below to complete this section and learning check.

| Step | Action |
|------|--------|
| 1 | Read the material in this section including the pages indicated in the resources section above. |
| 2 | Write down any notes or questions that you may wish to discuss with your instructor during your scheduled class. |
| 3 | Discuss any questions and/or concerns with your instructor. |
| 4 | Complete the learning in action, brain teaser and/or on-the-job activities presented by the instructor. |

## MONITORING AND CONTROLLING PROJECT WORK

Fill in the blanks with the correct descriptor

| Begin With | Organizational Process Assets |
|---|---|
| 1. Organizational Process Assets | |
| 2. Project Management Plan | **Project Management Plan** |
| 3. Performance Reports | **Performance Reports** |
| 4. Enterprise Environmental Factors | **Enterprise Environmental Factors** |
| **Method** | **Expert Judgment** |
| 1. Use Expert Judgment | |
| **Result** | **Change Requests** |
| 1. Change Requests | |
| 2. Project Management Plan Updates | **Project Management Plan Updates** |
| 3. Project Document Updates | **Project Document Updates** |

## PERFORM INTEGRATED CHANGE CONTROL

Fill in the blanks with the correct descriptor

| Begin With | Organizational Process Assets |
|---|---|
| 1. Organizational Process Assets | _____ _____ _____ |
| 2. Project Management Plan | **Project Management Plan** _____ _____ _____ |
| 3. Work Performance Information | **Work Performance Information** _____ _____ _____ |
| 4. Change Requests | **Change Requests** _____ _____ _____ |
| 5. Enterprise Environmental Factors | **Enterprise Environmental Factors** _____ _____ _____ |
| **Method** | |
| 1. Use Expert Judgment | **Expert Judgment** _____ _____ |
| 2. Change Control Meetings | **Change Control Meetings** _____ _____ _____ |

## PERFORM INTEGRATED CHANGE CONTROL CONT.

Fill in the blanks with the correct descriptor

| Result | Change Requests Status Updates |
|---|---|
| 1. Change Requests Status Updates | _____<br>_____<br>_____ |
| 2. Project Management Plan Updates | **Project Management Plan Updates**<br>_____<br>_____<br>_____ |
| 3. Project Document Updates | **Project Document Updates**<br>_____<br>_____<br>_____ |

## VERIFYING SCOPE

Fill in the blanks with the correct descriptor

| **Begin With** | **Requirements Documentation** |
|---|---|
| 1. Requirements Documentation | |
| 2. Project Management Plan | **Project Management Plan** |
| 3. Requirements Traceability Matrix | **Requirements Traceability Matrix** |
| 4. Validated Deliverables | **Validated Deliverables** |
| **Method** | **Inspection** |
| 1. Use Inspection | |
| **Result** | **Change Requests** |
| 1. Change Requests | |
| 2. Accepted Deliverables | **Accepted Deliverables** |
| 3. Project Document Updates | **Project Document Updates** |

## CONTROLLING SCOPE

Fill in the blanks with the correct descriptor

| Begin With | Requirements Documentation |
|---|---|
| 1. Requirements Documentation | _____<br>_____<br>_____ |
| 2. Project Management Plan | **Project Management Plan**<br>_____<br>_____<br>_____ |
| 3. Requirements Traceability Matrix | **Requirements Traceability Matrix**<br>_____<br>_____<br>_____<br>_____<br>_____<br>_____ |
| 4. Work Performance Information | **Work Performance Information**<br>_____<br>_____<br>_____ |
| 5. Organizational Process Assets | **Organization Process Assets**<br>_____<br>_____<br>_____ |
| Method | Variance Analysis |
| 1. Use Variance Analysis | _____<br>_____<br>_____<br>_____<br>_____ |

## CONTROLLING SCOPE CONT.

Fill in the blanks with the correct descriptor

| Result | |
|---|---|
| **1.** Work Performance Measurements | **Work Performance Measurements** <br><br><br> |
| **2.** Change Requests | **Change Requests** <br><br><br> |
| **3.** Project Document Updates | **Project Document Updates** <br><br> |
| **4.** Project Management Plan Updates | **Project Management Plan Updates** <br><br><br><br><br> |
| **5.** Organizational Process Assets Updates | **Organizational Process Assets Updates** <br><br><br><br><br> |

## SCHEDULE CONTROL

Fill in the blanks with the correct descriptor

| Begin With | Project Schedule |
|---|---|
| 1. Project Schedule | _____ <br> _____ <br> _____ |
| 2. Project Management Plan | **Project Management Plan** <br> _____ <br> _____ |
| 3. Work Performance Information | **Work Performance Information** <br> _____ <br> _____ |
| 4. Organizational Process Assets | **Organizational Process Assets** <br> _____ <br> _____ <br> _____ |
| **Method** | **Performance Reviews** |
| 1. Use Performance Reviews | _____ <br> _____ <br> _____ |
| 2. Variance Analysis | **Variance Analysis** <br> _____ <br> _____ |
| 3. Project Management Software | **Project Management Software** <br> _____ <br> _____ <br> _____ |
| 4. Resource Leveling | **Resource Leveling** <br> _____ <br> _____ <br> _____ |
| 5. What if Scenario Analysis | **What-if Scenario Analysis** <br> _____ <br> _____ <br> _____ |

## SCHEDULE CONTROL CONT.

Fill in the blanks with the correct descriptor

| Method | |
|---|---|
| 6. Adjusting Leads and Lags | **Adjusting Leads and Lags** <br>_____<br>_____<br>_____ |
| 7. Schedule Compression | **Schedule Compression** <br>_____<br>_____<br>_____<br>_____ |
| 8. Scheduling Tool | **Scheduling Tool** <br>_____<br>_____<br>_____<br>_____ |

| Result | |
|---|---|
| 1. Change Requests | **Change Requests** <br>_____<br>_____<br>_____<br>_____ |
| 2. Work Performance Measurements | **Work Performance Measurements** <br>_____<br>_____<br>_____ |
| 3. Project Document Updates | **Project Document Updates** <br>_____<br>_____<br>_____ |
| 4. Organizational Process Assets Updates | **Organizational Process Updates** <br>_____<br>_____ |
| 5. Project Management Plan Updates | **Project Management Plan Updates** <br>_____<br>_____ |

## COST CONTROL

Fill in the blanks with the correct descriptor

| Begin With | Project Funding Requirements |
|---|---|
| 1. Project Funding Requirements | |
| 2. Project Management Plan | **Project Management Plan** |
| 3. Work Performance Information | **Work Performance Information** |
| 4. Organizational Process Assets | **Organizational Process Assets** |
| Method | Performance Reviews |
| 1. Use Performance Reviews | |
| 2. Earned Value Management | **Earned Value Management** |
| 3. Forecasting | **Forecasting** |

## COST CONTROL CONT.

Fill in the blanks with the correct descriptor

| Method | To Complete Performance Index |
|---|---|
| 4. To Complete Performance Index | _____ _____ |
| 5. Variance Analysis | **Variance Analysis** _____ _____ |
| 6. Project Management Software | **Project Management Software** _____ _____ |
| **Result** | **Work Performance Measurements** |
| 1. Work Performance Measurements | _____ _____ |
| 2. Budget Forecasts | **Budget Forecasts** _____ _____ |
| 3. Organizational Process Assets Updates | **Organizational Process Assets Updates** _____ _____ |
| 4. Change Requests | **Change Requests** _____ _____ |
| 5. Project Management Plan Updates | **Project Management Plan Updates** _____ _____ |
| 6. Project Document Updates | **Project Document Updates** _____ _____ _____ _____ |

## QUALITY CONTROL

Fill in the blanks with the correct descriptor

| Begin With | Project Management Plan |
|---|---|
| 1. Project Management Plan | _____<br>_____<br>_____ |
| 2. Quality Metrics | **Quality Metrics**<br>_____<br>_____<br>_____<br>_____ |
| 3. Quality Checklists | **Quality Checklists**<br>_____<br>_____<br>_____<br>_____ |
| 4. Work Performance Measurements | **Work Performance Measurements**<br>_____<br>_____<br>_____<br>_____ |
| 5. Approved Change Requests | **Approved Change Requests**<br>_____<br>_____<br>_____<br>_____ |
| 6. Deliverables | **Deliverables**<br>_____<br>_____<br>_____<br>_____ |
| 7. Organizational Process Assets | **Organizational Process Assets**<br>_____<br>_____<br>_____<br>_____ |

## QUALITY CONTROL CONT.

Fill in the blanks with the correct descriptor

| Method | Cause and Effect Diagrams |
|---|---|
| 1. Use Cause and Effect Diagrams | _____ _____ |
| 2. Control Charts | **Control Charts** _____ _____ _____ _____ |
| 3. Flowcharting | **Flowcharting** _____ _____ _____ _____ |
| 4. Histogram | **Histogram** _____ _____ _____ _____ |
| 5. Pareto Chart | **Pareto Chart** _____ _____ _____ _____ |
| 6. Run Chart | **Run Chart** _____ _____ _____ |
| 7. Scatter Diagram | **Scatter Diagram** _____ _____ |
| 8. Statistical Sampling | **Statistical Sampling** _____ _____ _____ _____ |

## QUALITY CONTROL CONT.

Fill in the blanks with the correct descriptor

| Method | Inspection |
|---|---|
| 9. Inspection | |
| 10. Approved Change Requests Review | **Approved Change Requests Review** |

| Result | **Quality Control Measurements** |
|---|---|
| 1. Quality Control Measurements | |
| 2. Validated Changes | **Validated Changes** |
| 3. Validated Deliverables | **Validated Deliverables** |
| 4. Organizational Process Assets Updates | **Organizational Process Assets Updates** |
| 5. Change Requests | **Change Requests** |
| 6. Project Management Plan Updates | **Project Management Plan Updates** |
| 7. Project Document Updates | **Project Document Updates** |

## PERFORMANCE REPORTING

Fill in the blanks with the correct descriptor

| Begin With | |
|---|---|
| 1. Project Management Plan | **Project Management Plan**<br><br>_____<br>_____<br>_____ |
| 2. Work Performance Information | **Work Performance Information**<br><br>_____<br>_____<br>_____ |
| 3. Work Performance Measurements | **Work Performance Measurements**<br><br>_____<br>_____<br>_____ |
| 4. Budget Forecasts | **Budget Forecasts**<br><br>_____<br>_____ |
| 5. Organizational Process Assets | **Organizational Process Assets**<br><br>_____<br>_____<br>_____<br>_____ |
| **Method** | |
| 1. Use Variance Analysis | **Variance Analysis**<br><br>_____<br>_____ |
| 2. Forecasting Methods | **Forecasting Methods**<br><br>_____<br>_____ |
| 3. Communication Methods | **Communication Methods**<br><br>_____<br>_____ |
| 4. Reporting Systems | **Reporting Systems**<br><br>_____<br>_____<br>_____ |

## PERFORMANCE REPORTING CONT.

Fill in the blanks with the correct descriptor

| Result | Change Requests |
|---|---|
| 1. Change Requests | _____<br>_____<br>_____<br>_____ |
| 2. Organizational Process Assets Updates | **Organizational Process Assets Updates**<br>_____<br>_____<br>_____<br>_____ |
| 3. Performance Reports | **Performance Reports**<br>_____<br>_____<br>_____<br>_____ |

## MONITORING AND CONTROLLING RISK

Fill in the blanks with the correct descriptor

| **Begin With** | **Project Management Plan** |
|---|---|
| 1. Project Management Plan | _____ <br> _____ |
| 2. Work Performance Information | **Work Performance Information** <br> _____ <br> _____ |
| 3. Performance Reports | **Performance Reports** <br> _____ <br> _____ |
| 4. Risk Register | **Risk Register** <br> _____ <br> _____ |
| **Method** | **Risk Reassessment** |
| 1. Use Risk Reassessment | _____ <br> _____ |
| 2. Risk Audits | **Risk Audits** <br> _____ <br> _____ |
| 3. Variance and Trend Analysis | **Variance and Trend Analysis** <br> _____ <br> _____ |
| 4. Technical Performance | **Technical Performance** <br> _____ <br> _____ |
| 4. Reserve Analysis | **Reserve Analysis** <br> _____ <br> _____ |
| 5. Status Meeting | **Status Meeting** <br> _____ <br> _____ |

## MONITORING AND CONTROLLING RISK CONT.

Fill in the blanks with the correct descriptor

| Result | Risk Register Updates |
|---|---|
| 1. Risk Register Updates | _____<br>_____<br>_____<br>_____ |
| 2. Organizational Process Assets Updates | **Organizational Process Assets Updates**<br>_____<br>_____<br>_____<br>_____ |
| 3. Change Requests | **Change Requests**<br>_____<br>_____<br>_____<br>_____ |
| 4. Project Management Plan Updates | **Project Management Plan Updates**<br>_____<br>_____<br>_____<br>_____ |
| 5. Project Document Updates | **Project Document Updates**<br>_____<br>_____<br>_____<br>_____ |

## ADMINISTERING PROCUREMENTS

Fill in the blanks with the correct descriptor

| Begin With | Procurement Documents |
|---|---|
| 1. Procurement Documents | |
| 2. Project Management Plan | **Project Management Plan** |
| 3. Contract | **Contracts** |
| 4. Performance Reports | **Performance Reports** |
| 5. Approved Change Requests | **Approved Change Requests** |
| 6. Work Performance Information | **Work Performance Information** |

## ADMINISTERING PROCUREMENTS CONT.

Fill in the blanks with the correct descriptor

| Method | |
|---|---|
| | **Contract Change Control System** |
| 1. Use Contract Change Control System | _____ |
| 2. Procurement Performance Reviews | **Procurement Performance Reviews** _____ |
| 3. Inspections and Audits | **Inspections and Audits** _____ |
| 4. Performance Reporting | **Performance Reporting** _____ |
| 5. Payment Systems | **Payment Systems** _____ |
| 6. Claims Administration | **Claims Administration** _____ |
| 7. Records Management System | **Records Management System** _____ |

## ADMINISTERING PROCUREMENTS CONT.

Fill in the blanks with the correct descriptor

| Result | Procurement Documentation |
|--------|---------------------------|
| 1. Procurement Documentation | _____<br>_____<br>_____<br>_____ |
| 2. Organizational Process Assets Updates | **Organizational Process Assets Updates**<br>_____<br>_____<br>_____<br>_____ |
| 3. Change Requests | **Change Requests**<br>_____<br>_____<br>_____<br>_____ |
| 4. Project Management Plan Updates | **Project Management Plan Updates**<br>_____<br>_____<br>_____<br>_____ |

**explain the purpose of monitoring and controlling the project**

_____

_____

_____

_____

_____

**Describe the activities that take place in monitoring and controlling the project plan.**

_____

_____

_____

_____

_____

_____

_____

_____

_____

_____

**Explain the purpose of integrated change control and describe the activities that take place in this area.**

_____

_____

_____

_____

_____

_____

_____

_____

_____

_____

_____

_____

_____

**Explain the purpose of scope verification and scope control and describe what takes place in each of these areas.**

_____

_____

_____

_____

_____

**Explain why monitoring and controlling the project schedule is important.**

_____

_____

_____

_____

_____

**Explain why it is important to monitor and control cost in a project.**

_____

_____

_____

_____

_____

**State the purpose of performing quality control when monitoring and controlling the project.**

_____

_____

_____

_____

_____

**List the types of documents that may be needed to monitor and control the work of the project team.**

_____

_____

_____

_____

_____

**List and describe the type of documents that are produced for performance reporting as a part of managing and controlling the project plan.**

_____
_____
_____
_____
_____

**State the importance of managing communications to stakeholders.**

_____
_____
_____
_____
_____

**Explain the activities that take place as a part of risk monitoring and controlling.**

_____
_____
_____
_____
_____

**Explain the activities that take place as a part of contract administration.**

_____
_____
_____
_____

## LEARNING IN ACTION AND/OR ON-THE-JOB ACTIVITIES

The following is an activity that may be completed individually or as a small group. This activity is intended to assess your comprehension and application of the material that was previously covered. Answer the questions below and make some notes in the space provided.

Consider what happened on the last project that you were involved in or managed.

What factors contributed to the success of the project?

_____

_____

_____

_____

_____

_____

Which of the factors contributing to the success of the project relate to the concepts covered in this section?

_____

_____

_____

_____

_____

What tasks that relate to the material previously covered, helped you to successfully complete your project?

_____

_____

_____

_____

List and describe the areas of the project where you experienced challenges?

_____

_____

_____

_____

What factors contributed to this?

_____

_____

_____

_____

_____

Given what you learned about the areas covered in the previous section, what would you do differently in your next project?

_____

_____

_____

_____

_____

What tasks did you neglect that may have contributed to a more successful outcome?

_____

_____

_____

_____

_____

## THINGS THAT I NEED TO WORK ON

The following are things that I need to work on to be proficient in the concepts covered in this chapter.

_____

_____

_____

_____

_____

_____

_____

_____

_____

_____

# CLOSING AND PROFESSIONAL RESPONSIBILITY

## AFTER STUDYING THIS CHAPTER, YOU SHOULD BE ABLE TO

- describe the project closeout process.
- list the three reasons why projects end.
- describe the four types of project endings.
- list some things that must take place in project closing.

## AS YOU READ THIS CHAPTER, BE SURE THAT YOU UNDERSTAND THE FOLLOWING TERMS AND IDEAS.

- Project Closeout
- Starvation
- Integration
- Extinction
- Addition

## REQUIREMENTS TO COMPLETE SECTION

To successfully complete this section, you must
- complete the learning check
- complete the learning in action requirements
- complete the on-the-job activities, and
- answer brain teaser questions assigned by instructor.

## TIME REQUIRED

This section is included as a part of unit six. Two weeks is allotted for successful completion of unit six.

## SIGN-OFF

Sign off for this section will be completed by the instructor.

## RESOURCES

The following outlines the resources that you will need to complete this section
- PMBOK Guide fourth edition, sections 4.6 and 12.4.
- PMI Code of Ethics and Professional Conduct.
- Heldman, fifth edition chapter 12.

## INSTRUCTIONS

Follow the steps below to complete this section and learning check.

| Step | Action |
|------|--------|
| 1 | Read the material in this section including the pages indicated in the resources section above. |
| 2 | Write down any notes or questions that you may wish to discuss with your instructor during your scheduled class. |
| 3 | Discuss any questions and/or concerns with your instructor. |
| 4 | Complete the learning in action, brain teaser and/or on-the-job activities presented by the instructor. |

## CLOSE PROJECT

Fill in the blanks with the correct descriptor

| Begin With | Accepted Deliverables |
|---|---|
| 1. Accepted Deliverables | _____<br>_____ |
| 2. Project Management Plan | **Project Management Plan**<br>_____<br>_____<br>_____ |
| 3. Organizational Process Assets | **Organizational Process Assets**<br>_____<br>_____<br>_____<br>_____ |
| **Method** | **Expert Judgment** |
| 1. Use Expert Judgment | _____<br>_____<br>_____ |
| **Result** | **Final Product, Service or Result Transition** |
| 1. Final Product, Service or Result Transition | _____<br>_____<br>_____ |
| 2. Organizational Process Assets Updates | **Organizational Process Assets Updates**<br>_____<br>_____<br>_____ |

## CLOSE PROCUREMENTS

Fill in the blanks with the correct descriptor

| Begin With | Procurement Documentation |
|---|---|
| 1. Procurement Documentation | _____<br>_____<br>_____ |
| 2. Project Management Plan | **Project Management Plan**<br>_____<br>_____<br>_____<br>_____ |
| **Method** | **Procurement Audits** |
| 1. Use Procurement Audits | _____<br>_____<br>_____ |
| 2. Negotiated Settlements | **Negotiated Settlements**<br>_____<br>_____<br>_____ |
| 3. Records Management System | **Records Management System**<br>_____<br>_____<br>_____<br>_____ |
| **Result** | **Closed Procurements** |
| 1. Closed Procurements | _____<br>_____ |
| 2. Organizational Process Assets Updates | **Organizational Process Assets Updates**<br>_____<br>_____<br>_____ |

**Describe the project closeout process.**

_____

_____

_____

_____

_____

**List the three reasons why projects end.**

_____

_____

_____

_____

_____

**Describe the four types of project endings.**

_____

_____

_____

_____

_____

_____

_____

_____

_____

_____

_____

_____

_____

**.List some things that must take place in project closing.**

_____

_____

_____

_____

_____

_____

_____

_____

_____

## LEARNING IN ACTION AND/OR ON-THE-JOB ACTIVITIES

The following is an activity that may be completed individually or as a small group. This activity is intended to assess your comprehension and application of the material that was previously covered. Answer the questions below and make some notes in the space provided.

Consider what happened on the last project that you were involved in or managed.

What factors contributed to the success of the project?

_____

_____

_____

_____

_____

Which of the factors contributing to the success of the project relate to the concepts covered in this section?

_____

_____

_____

_____

_____

What tasks that relate to the material previously covered, helped you to successfully complete your project?

_____

_____

_____

_____

_____

List and describe the areas of the project where you experienced challenges?

_____

_____

_____

_____

_____

What factors contributed to this?

_____

_____

_____

_____

_____

Given what you learned about the areas covered in the previous section, what would you do differently in your next project?

_____

_____

_____

_____

What tasks did you neglect that may have contributed to a more successful outcome?

_____

_____

_____

_____

## THINGS THAT I NEED TO WORK ON

The following are things that I need to work on to be proficient in the concepts covered in this chapter.

_____

_____

_____

_____

_____

_____

_____

_____

_____

_____

# BRAIN TEASER EXERCISES

# Brain Teaser Exercises

## Earned Value Analysis

1. You're working on a 5 month project. You've budgeted $12,000 per month. At the end of month 2 you are 30% complete and have spent $30,000. What is your BAC?
   - $12,000
   - $60,000
   - Not enough information
   - $14,500

2. You're working on a 5 month project. You've budgeted $12,000 per month. At the end of month 2 you are 30% complete and have spent $30,000. What is your Earned Value?
   - 2 months
   - $24,000
   - $60,000
   - $18,000

3. You're working on a 5 month project. You've budgeted $12,000 per month. At the end of month 2 you are 30% complete and have spent $30,000. What is your CPI?
   - $18,000
   - .8
   - 1.2
   - .6

4. You're working on a 5 month project. You've budgeted $12,000 per month. At the end of month 2 you are 30% complete and have spent $30,000. What is your SPI?
   - .75
   - 1.33
   - Not enough information
   - .3

5. You're working on a 5 month project. You've budgeted $12,000 per month. At the end of month 3 you are 30% complete and have spent $30,000. What is your schedule variance?
- -$18,000
- .8
- 1.2
- -$6,000

6. You're working on a 5 month project. You've budgeted $12,000 per month. At the end of month 3 you are 40% complete and have spent $30,000. What is your CV?
- + $6,000
- - $6,000
- Not enough information
- .6

7. You're working on a 5 month project. You've budgeted $12,000 per month. At the end of month 3 you are 30% complete and have spent $30,000. The first few months had a lot of things go wrong, which you don't think will occur again. What is your ETC? What is your EAC?


8. You hire someone to paint a room with 4 walls. Each wall takes 2 days and costs $100.00 to paint. He is 25% done and you have paid him $150.00. What is the CV? What is the CPI? What is the EAC? What is the ETC? What is the VAC?

## CRITICAL PATH

Review the project schedule below and answer the following questions.

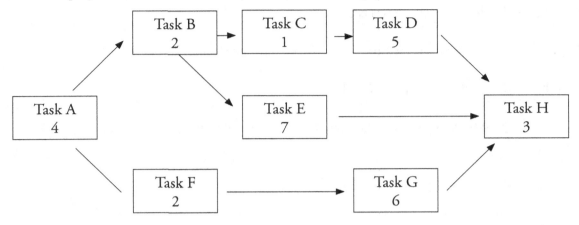

1. What is the critical path of the project?

2. How much float is on task E?

3. What is the duration of the project?

4. How much slack does task D have?

5. If activity D is delayed by 2 days, what is the effect on the project?

## FLOAT

**The chart below describes a network diagram.  Draw that diagram and answer the questions.**

| Task | Predecessor | ES | EF | LS | LF |
|------|-------------|----|----|----|----|
| A | ST | 1 | 3 | 1 | 3 |
| B | ST | 1 | 2 | 2 | 3 |
| C | A,B | 4 | 6 | 6 | 8 |
| D | B | 3 | 4 | 4 | 5 |
| E | C, D | 9 | 9 | 10 | 10 |

1. What is the critical path?

2. What is the duration of the project?

3. What is the free float on task B?

4. What is the total float of pay ST-B-D-E?

5. What is the only way to calculate float in a network diagram.

## DECISION TREE ANALYSIS & EMV

You need to decide whether to hire a new marketing firm to supplement your current team downstairs. The new firm costs money ($50K), but estimates indicate that they should generate more sales for you (60% chance of getting $1m; 40% chance of earning $200K) than your current team (60% chance of getting $600K; 40% chance of getting $400K). To get an answer, you build a decision tree.

- Based on the decision tree, which way should you go?
- What would be the answer if the new firm costs rose to $100,000?

## BASIC PROBABILITY

Before starting, it is important to remember that all events have to equal 1.0 or 100%. Therefore, if there is a 70% chance that something will happen, then there must be a 30% chance that it will **not** happen.

*A. You have to get the project charter done (80% chance) as well as get project approval of it by your boss (60% chance) by September, before moving to the planning stage.*

*B. The senior boss has said that as long as you either get the charter done, or your immediate boss approves the project, by September, you can move to do the planning.*

## STANDARD DEVIATION, PERT AND VARIANCE

You are the PM of a new project and the boss has asked that you provide a time estimate for its completion. You have talked to your team and they have said that if everything goes well then it might take 3 months. However, if problems arise - 12 months. Most likely though is that it will take 6 months.

1. What is the PERT estimate of the project's duration?

2. What is the standard deviation of the estimate?

3. It is a very important project so we must be 95% accurate. Therefore, what is the range that fits this level of accuracy?

## SHARE RATIOS AND CONTRACTS

1.  Under the original contract with a vendor, you had agreed to a cost plus incentive fee contract with the expected cost being $200,000, a fee of $40,000 and a share ratio of 60/40. In the end the work was done well and the final costs were $180,000. How much do you pay the vendor?

2.  If the actual costs are $210,000, how much does the seller receive?

3.  You signed a fixed price plus contract with the target price being $250,000, the target profit being $50,000, a ceiling price of $300,000 and a share ratio of 40/60. The actual costs turn out to be $200,000. What do you pay the seller?

4.  In the above scenario, what do you pay the seller if the costs rise to $280,000?

5.  Based on the original contract, what is the point of total assumption?

## GENERAL CATEGORY

1.   You are part way through a project and have spent $400 on labor. You have to spend another $300 to finish and the project will earn you $500. What are the sunk costs? Should you continue?

2.   You hire someone to paint a room with four walls. Each wall takes $25 in paint and $50 in labor, and brushes cost $75 for the whole job. What are the variable costs for the project? What are the fixed costs?

3.   A company has four projects with expected costs of $50, $75, $80, and $100. The manager splits an administrative fee of $100 across all the projects for supplies and her salary. What are the direct and indirect costs for each project?

4.   What are two types of parametric estimating?

5.   What is the process of taking into account all pre and post project costs in making a selection?

6.   Adding 50% more resources but only getting 10% more production obeys which law?

7.   What is the name of a technique used to find less costly ways of doing the same work?

8.   What is another way of describing internal and external failure costs that may include rework, loss of reputation etc.

9.   What is a term to describe a characteristic in someone who does not like risk?

10.   How would you describe a good or bad occurrence that can affect the project?

11.   How would you describe uncertainty?

12.   What is the name of the document that describes how to approach and plan for risk activities on a project?

13.   What are some sources of risk on a project?

14.   What are some risk identification techniques?

15. What is risk tolerance?

16. What is the numerical analysis of the risks on a project?

17. What are some examples of risk categories?

18. What are two types of risk?

19. What might you call something that indicates that a risk event might happen?

20. What is a subjective analysis of risk?

21. What should you do before using risk information and plan responses?

22. What are the main outputs of qualitative risk analysis?

23. What is a primary difference in outputs between qualitative and quantitative risk analysis?

24. Who helps develop the risk response and takes responsibility for the risk?

25. What are some common risk response strategies?

26. What do you call the amount of time/cost you set aside for risks?

27. What is the process for examining the effectiveness of the risk response plan?

28. What is an unplanned response to unidentified risk?

29. What are strategies for addressing positive risks or opportunities?

30. What is the technique used to calculate contingency on a project?

31. Document reviews and diagramming techniques are tools of which risk process?

32. What is the name of the document that does not show when people will do their jobs only their roles and responsibilities?

33. What document shows resources used in a bar chart format?

34. What is the name of the plan for managing staff after they are identified?

35. What is the preferred technique to solve problems on a project?

36. What is a management technique that involves pushing one viewpoint over another?

37. What is the definition of power based on personality or link to someone in a higher position?

38. What is the definition of power based on position?

39. What theory suggests that people do not work only for security or money, they also want to use their skills or achieve success?

40. What is the name of the technique that is used to emphasize agreement between parties rather than differences. This technique does not result in a decision.

41. What is the name of a technique that rarely solves long term conflicts and involves the two sides walking away from the issue?

42. What is the name of a leadership style that focuses on problem solving in a group that may or may not be useful?

43. What is the name of the theory that suggests that staff will work hard for good performance so that they will be rewarded?

44. What is a very useful team building tool that involves the team defining the scope of the project?

45. What is the name of the theory that suggests that working conditions can only destroy motivation not improve it?

46. What are some areas that are typically major sources of conflict on a project?

47. What is the definition of a perception that a person is good or bad in all things just because of their work in one area?

48. What is the name of the theory that suggests that workers/managers either dislike and or are indifferent to their work; or like to work and will do it well?

49. What is the definition of some destructive roles on a project?

50. What is the definition of some constructive roles on a project?

51. What is the definition of quality?

52. What is the name of the term for giving little extras to the customer (this is not recommended by PMI).

53. What is the definition of marginal analysis?

54. What is the definition of mutually exclusive?

55. What are cost of non conformance to quality?

56. What is the term used for looking at past projects to get a measure/metric to compare the current project's performance?

57. What is the definition of variable sampling?

58. What is the definition of attribute sampling?

59. What is the definition of Kaizen?

60. What is the definition of Design of Experiments?

61. What is the cost of quality?

62. What is a force field analysis?

63. What information is represented on a milestone chart?

64. What is the shortest route to complete the entire project that represents no float?

65. What is the name of a hierarchical structure of the resources by category and type?

66. What is a Gantt chart used for?

67. What is the term used for compressing a schedule but usually results in increased costs?

68. What is the term used to describe the amount of time that a task can be delayed without delaying the early start date of its successor?

69. What is the definition of variance analysis?

70. What is a Monte Carlo Simulation?

71. What is an external dependency?

72. What is the definition of a lag?

73. What is the definition of a critical path?

74. What is the definition of the term fast tracking?

75. What is the amount of time that a task may be delayed without hurting the scheduled end date of the project?

76. What is the result of resource leveling?

77. What is resources analysis used for?

78. What are other names for mandatory and discretionary dependencies?

79. What is the name of the method used to create different scenarios with the network diagram to see the impact on the schedule?

80. Analogous, parametric and three-point estimates are tools and techniques of what process?

81. During which process would you apply lags and leads?

82. During which phase of the project can a stakeholder have the greatest influence of cost, quality and schedule?

83. Planned revision of the project plan during the project uses what type of planning?

84. How do you define the triple constraint and what effect does the triple constraint have on projects?

85. What is the disadvantage of projectized organizations?

86. What is the name for the project manager in a functional or a weak matrix organization respectively?

87. What is the main disadvantage in a balanced matrix organization?

88. What is the main disadvantage of a strong matrix organization?

89. What is the name of the tool that gathers, integrates and disseminates outputs of project management processes?

90. What is the purpose of a work authorization system?

91. What is the purpose of the configuration management system?

92. What is the purpose of lessons learned or post mortem and when is this process completed?

93. What are four ways that a project can end?

94. What is a negative impact on team members from working in foreign countries? Training helps to mitigate this.

95. What is the name of the person or organization who will use the product of the project? These are often several layers or groups.

96. What are three characteristics of a project?

97. What is a deliverables orientated grouping of project components?

98. What is the difference between scope verification and quality control?

99. What is the lowest level of the WBS?

100. What is the name and description of the two different types of scope?

101. What are two methods of alternatives identification?

102. What are four different ways to organize a WBS?

103. What is the hierarchical list of items needed for a product?

104. What is the result of uncontrolled scope changes?

105. What results in changes to the scope baseline?

106. What is the name of out of scope extras included by the team that is not recommended by PMI?

107. What is the rule of thumb (heuristic) for how long work packages should be?

108. What is the name of the tool that helps define the WBS by reusing work from a similar project?

109. What is used to describe the work package in greater detail?

# RESOURCES

Heldman, K. *PMP Project Management Professional Exam Study Guide*, 5th ed. Wiley Publishing, Inc., 2007.

Project Management Institute. *A Guide to the Project Management Body of Knowledge*: PMBOK Guide, 4th ed. Project Management Institute, 2008.